They All Sat Down

Pianists in Profile

by

Leonice Thompson Kidd

The Willis Music Company, Florence, Kentucky

11680E

CREDITS

DOVER PUBLICATIONS, INC.: James Canmer, *Great Composers In Historic Photographs* (Bartók, MacDowell), *Great Instrumentalists In Historic Photographs* (Clara Schumann, Moscheles, Leschetizky); Amy Fay, *Music Study In Germany*; Gilbert Chase, *The Music Of Spain*

RANDOM HOUSE, INC.: *Letters Of Felix Mendelssohn*, ed. by Gisela Seldon-Goth; Lawrence and Elizabeth Hanson, *Prokofiev*

ALFRED A. KNOPF, INC., Erich Schenk, *Mozart And His Times*, trans. by Richard and Clara Winston; Herbert Weinstock, *Chopin: The Man And His Music*; Walter Niemann, *Brahms*, trans. by Catherine Alison Phillips

DODD, MEAD & COMPANY, INC.: Robert Haven Schauffler, *The Unknown Brahms*; Henry T. Finck, *Grieg And His Music*

HARPER AND ROW, PUBLISHERS, INC.: Victor Seroff, *A Soviet Tragedy* (Funk & Wagnalls)

TAPLINGER PUBLISHING CO., INC.: J. Ujfalussy, *Béla Bartók*

SIMON & SCHUSTER, INC.: *The Great Pianists*, copyright 1963, 1987 by Harold C. Schonberg, copyright renewed 1991 by Harold C. Schonberg, reprinted by permission of Simon & Schuster, Inc.

WILLIAM HEINEMANN LIMITED: *The Selected Correspondence Of Fryderyk Chopin,* trans. and ed. by Arthur Hedley, reprinted by permission of William Heinemann Limited

To the memory of my favorite pianist,

My Mother

CONTENTS

PRELUDE: a *gravicembalo col piano e forte* is born

CODA

ILLUSTRATIONS

Cover: Student (Lisa Floyd) with Mozart and Liszt

FOREWORD

Who were these unknown men and women who wrote and played the piano music which today's student hopes to re-create? When and where did they live, how did they fit into the musical life of their time and how did their life affect and change the world of music? All too often these questions about the brilliant people who gave us such wonderful piano music are never raised and an important aspect of the student's musical learning and understanding has been neglected.

Piano pedagogy has undergone a remarkable transformation in the last fifty years. An increased understanding of the psychology and various modes of learning has resulted in many fine materials tailored to meet the special needs of the young student. Enlightened pedagogy today recognizes the importance of developing a comprehensive musical background including some study of theory and music history. Despite the addition of historical information in a number of today's repertoire books, there remains a genuine need for a book that deals exclusively with the historical and biographical material of our musical tradition.

They All Sat Down, with its charming vignettes of some of the world's great piano personalities, is a welcome answer to this need. The author's easy-to-read narrative prose, avoidance of pedantics and relaxed and witty style make this book especially appealing. The many anecdotes about past and present pianists/composers whet the appetite for continued study of these fascinating people. This is a book that will open doors to a life-long study of the piano and help build enlightened audiences of the future.

Margaret Lorince
Professor Emeritus, West Virginia University
Immediate Past President, Music Teachers National Association

INTRODUCTION

Knowing about the players in any sport makes the game more interesting for the spectator. Knowing about the composer of a piece of music makes that music more exciting to hear. It should also add to the joy of practicing it, thus creating a desirable condition for student and teacher alike.

The personal portraits, tinted with direct quotations, are designed to reveal the human qualities of these famous musicians who started out as pianists. They are brought to life at the keyboard, giving young people something with which to identify. New dimension is added to the music and, perhaps most important of all, chronology is established. Concocted as appetizers, the profiles are offered as stimulus to further reading.

I confess to falling in love with all these talented human beings. I hope it turns out that way for the reader.

L. T. K.

ACKNOWLEDGEMENTS

This book has sustained an extended development, with many *da capos,* repeats, *ritardandos*, rests, and, at the end, an *accelerando*. Much is owed to many. Most is owed to Roger Wiley, without whom the work might never have been programmed. James Bastien, Judy Delton and her St. Paul group, and Dr. George Lucktenberg have all contributed time and effort. Suggestions and encouragement have come from Dr. Maurice Hinson, Dr. Irene Grau, Clara Mitchell Ekwurtzel, Pat Leonard, Jan Strootman, the late Kay Gerster, John Goodbody, Lynn Freeman Olson, and numerous other colleagues, editors, and friends.

A special bow goes to the living composers who responded to my plea for news of current activities, to Charleston County reference librarians, and to all those piano students who were my first critics.

PRELUDE

[a gravicembalo col piano e forte is born]

Most musical instruments, like music itself, have grown up gradually, by the littles. Some started out quite simply. For example, the piano's first great-great-great grandfather was a string that "sang" when plucked.

Another ancestor of the piano is the lyre. According to Greek mythology, a god named Hermes made one of these instruments from the shell of a tortoise. One day he found himself feeling guilty because he had stolen some oxen from Apollo, one of the other gods. He decided to give him his lyre as a peace offering. Apollo practiced and learned how to play so well that he became known as "the god of music."

Among human beings, the greatest performer on the lyre was Orpheus. He came by his talent naturally, for his mother belonged to a group of singing sisters called "The Muses," and he grew up in Thrace, where lived the most musical people in all of Greece. Animals, trees, even rocks are said to have followed him when he played.

Other ancient stringed instruments include the cithara, the harp, the lute, and the guitar. The strings of these are plucked either by the fingers or a pick. Performers hold a mallet or leather-covered hammer in each fist to strike the strings of a dulcimer. This instrument the Germans often called the "Hackbrett," meaning the "chopping-board."

The dulcimer so impressed a certain Pantaleon Hebenstreit that he decided to design his own. It developed into a veritable giant: six feet long, two soundboards, a range of five octaves, and nearly two hundred strings. The ends of each of the two mallets were covered with different materials so that he could play loudly or softly--or in between. His swelling arpeggios on unstopped strings were said to be sensational. When he played for the king of France in 1705, this monarch suggested he name the instrument for himself. Later, even some pianofortes were sometimes called *pantaleons*.

With the invention of the clavichord and the harpsichord, direct contact between the player and the strings was eliminated. Keys were introduced as "go-betweens." The clavichord, probably the first stringed instrument with a keyboard, made its appearance before the end of the fourteenth century. Lowering the front of a key caused a metal blade called a "tangent" to rise at the other end and strike the string, producing a sweet, soft tone. A German poet described the clavichord as an "instrument of solitude, of melancholy, of inexpressible sweetness. ... He who does not like noise, outburst, tumult . . . will turn away from the harpsichord and the fortepiano and will choose a clavichord."

The harpsichord produces a stronger, more metallic sound than the clavichord. Strings in early harpsichords were plucked by quills of crow or raven feathers. Later instruments often had two keyboards; a few experimental models had three. Harpsichords came in many shapes. Some appeared delicate, like miniature grand pianos on stilts. Some were heavy looking, as though they were wearing wooden skirts. Many were elaborately decorated with paintings and carvings.

Near the end of the seventeenth century, Prince Ferdinand de Medici persuaded the harpsichord maker of Padua, Italy, to move to Florence to take care of his many harpsichords and spinets. Bartolommeo Cristofori did some experimenting in his spare time. Around the year 1700, he gave birth to what he christened a *gravicembalo col piano e forte* (harpsichord with soft and loud). It has a range of four and a half octaves, and the strings are struck with hammers. As the name implies, it can be played softly or loudly. The inventor built about twenty of these instruments, at least three of which are still in existence. One is in New York City's Metropolitan Museum. The others hold court in Rome and Leipzig.

A description of Cristofori's invention appeared in a Venetian journal in 1711. Fourteen years later, this article was translated into German and published in a Dresden newspaper. Not long afterwards, an organ builder living near Dresden, Gottfried Silbermann, started to construct fortepianos in Germany.

By the 1700s, pianos, as though they were kites in the spring, were popping up everywhere. Johann Andreas Stein built them in Augsburg, and Anton Walther built them in Vienna. Sebastian Erard built pianos in France, Johannes Zumpe and John Broadwood built them in England, and Johann Behrend built pianos in Philadelphia. "Everybody plays; everybody learns music," reported a German periodical. Over three hundred piano teachers lived in the city of Vienna.

The early pianos were not similar to the ones we know today. At first, they resembled harpsichords in appearance, with a range of about five octaves. In 1777 a special six-octave piano was built for England's music historian, Dr. Charles Burney. It allowed his two daughters to sit at the piano and play duets while wearing hoop skirts. Eventually, pianos came in more shapes and sizes than Alice in her trip through Wonderland. The most popular were the squares, uprights, grands, giraffes, and pyramids (sometimes complete with clocks).

The framework of the first pianos was made of wood, instead of the iron now used. The tone was light, and hammers and strings frequently broke. Hand levers, used to create a damping effect similar to that achieved by Hebenstreit, were replaced by knee-action pedals. Foot pedals were finally introduced in England. At the opening of the nineteenth century, there were two types of pianos used by professionals: the German, or Viennese, with its flute-like tone and easy action, and the English, with a fuller tone and heavier action.

In 1840, Jonas Chickering of Boston obtained a patent for the complete cast-iron frame used for his concert grands. A few years later, Heinrich Englehardt Steinweg came to America from Germany and founded the firm of Steinway & Sons. The famous opera composer Rossini described the Steinway pianos as "great as thunder and storm, and sweet as the fluting of a nightingale on a Spring night."

By the beginning of the twentieth century, over two hundred piano manufacturers were plying their craft in the U.S.A. From Maine to

California, pianos were being carried into homes; and mature musicians, amateurs, and young neophytes were sitting down at their keyboards.

Cristofori piano (1720), The Metropolitan Museum of Art
The Crosby Brown Collection of Musical Instruments (1889)

1. THE BACHS

The first Bach boy to show musical ability was born about one hundred years before the Pilgrims stepped onto Plymouth Rock. By 1720, at least thirty Bachs occupied positions of importance in the world of music. In fact, the name "Bach" had come to mean "musician": musical groups were frequently called "the Bachs," although there might have been no member of the Bach family in the groups.

Johann Sebastian Bach was the greatest musician of all the Bachs--some say of the entire world. When he visited Dresden in 1736, he tried out some of Silbermann's pianos. Bach approved of the tone, but he felt the action was too stiff, the upper register too weak. Annoyed by this criticism, Silbermann is said to have been "angry with Mr. Bach for a long time." But after thinking it over, he may have decided that Bach was right, for he corrected these very defects.

Ten years later, Bach visited his son, Carl Philipp Emanuel Bach, harpsichordist at the court of Frederick the Great in Berlin. He barely had time to meet his daughter-in-law and greet his new grandson before being summoned by His Majesty. Frederick the Great, who played the flute and owned fifteen Silbermann pianos, led the great Bach from room to room, asking him to improvise on each of the fortepianos. This time, Bach expressed his approval of the instruments, although he had little time left in which to adapt his technique to them.

J.S. Bach did have his finger in the pie in one way: he one of the first to emphasize the importance of using the thumb. (Right hand ascending scales had been played with third and fourth fingers, and descending with second and third. This fingering was called "Bach's fingering" in Germany.) Bach's principles were disseminated by son Carl, who published *Essay on the True Art of Playing Keyboard Instruments.* Clementi wrote of this Bible for budding performers, "Whatever I know of fingering and the new style . . . whatever I understand of the pianoforte I learned from this book."

The other son to figure in the development of the piano was Johann Christian Bach. Like his brothers, he received his first lesson at the age of nine, parrying the pitfalls of the difficult *Well-Tempered Clavier.* Youngest of the Bach boys, he was fifteen when his father died, leaving him three pedalled claviers, some linen shirts, and a talent for music.

Johann Christian soon moved to Berlin to live with his half-brother Carl, then thrirty-six years old. Here he would be exposed to his brother's clavier and composition lessons, daily concerts, and all those Silbermann pianos.

The concerts included opera on Monday and Friday nights in the opera house built by Frederick the Great. The king attended most of the productions, standing behind the leader and following the score on a music stand. He listened for wrong notes and reprimanded the responsible musician as if he were, according to one writer, "a generalissimo in the field." With or without errors, the operas fascinated the young Bach.

At the age of twenty, Johann Christian left for Italy. In Bologna he studied with the famous scholar Padre Martini. He composed church music and served as organist of the Milan Cathedral, at the same time writing several operas. These attracted attention outside Italy, and in 1762, Johann Christian became composer for the King's Theatre in London.

Later, he assumed the position formerly held by Handel, that of Music Master to the Queen of England. He gave harpsichord lessons to the queen, accompanied when the king played the flute, and taught their many children.

London was quickly becoming a city of music. Concerts took place in taverns, in the bandstands of the many public gardens, and in the city's first concert hall. The hall, called "Hickford's Room," held two hundred people and presented such novelties as the guitar, musical glasses, a troupe of trained cats who "howled on cue," and performers who played the harp with one hand and the harpsichord with the other.

Pianos had been introduced into England from Germany a few years before Bach arrived there. He soon began to write for the instrument. Burney describes some of his piano compositions as being "such as ladies can execute with little trouble." Johann Christian had spent more of his time in Italy drawing notes on manuscript paper than he had practicing the harpsichord, crippling his hand in two ways. Since he played what he wrote, his piano pieces exhibited no great technical advance, although they often sounded more difficult than they were. This fact may have helped his ratings with students. His preference for the new instrument inspired the manufacturers to work at improving the piano, so, because of him, piano manufacturing progressed more quickly in England than it did anywhere else.

On June 2, 1768, John Bach (he now used the English version of his name) became the first to perform a solo in public on the new pianoforte. He played one of his own compositions on a "square" instrument built by Johannes Zumpe. The concert took place in the Large Room of a tavern called "The Thatched House."

Bach had already established himself as a performer by giving series concerts with a viola da gamba player, Carl Abel. Each year, they gave fifteen concerts that presented compositions by both men and included various guest artists. For a while, they held their programs in Carlisle House, a mansion in the Soho District owned by a lady who offered "tea below stairs and ventilators above." This took care of any complaints of too much heat, "without subjecting the subscribers to the least danger of catching cold."

Eventually, these concerts, which continued until Bach's death, were moved to a handsome new hall in Hanover Square. Statues and paintings by Cipriani and Gainsborough adorned the room. In a letter to her son, one subscriber wrote: " 'Tis a great stroke of Bach's to entertain the town so elegantly."

As a matter of fact, the hall seemed almost too decorative, and statues of Apollo and the Muses were removed from the stage after a few weeks. When one of the patrons noticed their absence, she exclaimed to Bach, "What! Apollo and the Muses gone?" Bach replied, "They have quitted their late station, Madame, but have not absolutely deserted us. When the performance begins, I hope your ladyship will hear them all."

At the age of thirty-eight, John Bach married Cecilia Grassi, who had sung the "first woman's part" at the opera. An excellent musician, she helped her husband in many ways. According to one writer she was "rather *passée* for a *prima donna*," but someone else commented that her voice sounded well on the water.

The English nobility often celebrated important events with water parties on the Thames. Music usually played an important role, the most famous example being Handel's *Water Music*. Bach spent many hours cruising the river on a decked yacht and arranging various concerts for gala celebrations.

In addition to writing music that was to be played on the water, John Bach wrote operas, chamber music, church music, more than forty symphonies, and clavier compositions--including concertos, sonatas, and duets. He sometimes played his duets in public with a six-year-old child prodigy who later became the famous Mrs. Billington, noted for charm and beauty as well as an exceptional voice.

Much of John Bach's life in England was a glamorous one. For several years, he was considered the country's leading musician. Padre Martini honored him by requesting a portrait for his collection, and the distinguished Thomas Gainsborough painted it. Bach received an invitation to write an opera in honor of the birthday of the Elector at Mannheim, where the orchestra and singers were considered the best in Europe. He was commissioned to write an opera to be performed in Paris. When his brother Friedrich and his eighteen-year-old nephew came for a visit, Bach took them to hear one of his operas. And, he persuaded his brother to invest in a piano.

Unfortunately, John Bach, so talented at managing notes, did not manage money as well. The expensive new hall added to his financial burdens. After a few years, the fickle public turned its attention to a younger performer and teacher. Finally, he was robbed by a housekeeper. These adversities probably contrubuted to his death at the age of forty-six. Bach left many debts and was buried without fanfare. Not many attended the benefit concert for his widow, but the queen granted her a pension that enabled her to return to her native Italy. Even death could not erase the contribution made by Johann Christian Bach to the development and promotion of the instrument called the piano.

Square pianoforte by Johannes Zumpe,
London, 1767, Victoria and Albert Museum

The Grand Tour and Environs

2. WOLFGANG AMADEUS MOZART: The Prodigy

Four years before his debut as a piano soloist, John Bach sat at the harpsichord with an eight-year-old boy between his knees. For two hours they made music--first one and then the other--while the King and Queen of England looked on and listened in amazement.

The boy was Wolfgang Amadeus Mozart. He had entered the world on a wintry day in January of 1756 in the picturesque town of Salzburg, Austria. Here he shared a fourth floor apartment with his father and mother, his sister Marianne, a servant named Theresa, a canary, and a dog called "Bimperl."

Wolfgang's father, Leopold, worked for the Archbishop of Salzburg. He played violin in the court orchestra, trained choir boys, taught violin and clavier, and composed music. Some of his compositions showed considerable imagination: they ranged from a "sleigh-ride piece with five sleigh bells" to pieces that used the lyre, bagpipes, dulcimer, or rifles. His most important accomplishment may have been a book on how to play the violin. Published in 1756, it soon appeared in several languages.

When barely three years old, Wolfgang began to eavesdrop on his sister's clavier lessons. As soon as his father finished his instruction, the child would rush to the instrument and try to play. He took particular delight in picking out thirds and listening to them. Within a year, he started to learn the pieces in Marianne's notebook. Each one he apparently mastered in about half an hour, frequently between 9:00 and 9:30 in the evening.

Musicians came and went at the Mozart house, usually with music tucked under their arms. Andreas Schactner, the court trumpeter, was one of the most frequent guests. In reminiscing about Wolfgang's childhood he wrote that "even his childish foolery and games with toys had to be accompanied by music if they were to interest him. When we . . . carried toys for a game from one room to another, whichever of us was empty-handed had to sing and fiddle a march. . . ."

The boy particularly admired the tone of Schactner's violin, which he called a "butter-fiddle." One day Schactner let him try out the instrument. When he visited the Mozarts a day or so later, he found the young lad fiddling on his own violin. After asking, "How is your butter-fiddle?" Wolfgang said, "Herr Schactner, your violin is tuned half a quarter tone lower than mine if you left it tuned as it was when I last played on it." The older man laughed, but when he checked, he found this to be true.

One day Schactner and Leopold discovered the four-year-old writing what he called "a concerto for the clavier." Childish ink blots spattered the page, but the notes were correct and orderly. The only problem, according to Leopold, seemed to be that it would be too difficult to play. The child responded to this criticism, "That's why it's called a concerto. You have to practice it until you can do it. See, this is how it ought to go." And he managed to give a general idea of what he had in mind.

Problems in arithmetic held a special fascination for Wolfgang. He covered the walls, the chairs, and the floors with figures written in chalk. And it didn't necessarily have to be his own house that he so adorned. According to his sister, "Many a threat, and many a chastising did he receive before his zeal was checked."

Interest in math continued for several years. One of his many letters --written from Italy at the age of thirteen--requests that his arithmetic book be sent to him. He signed the letter, "Friend of the League of Numbers."

In 1762, Leopold took the two children to Munich, where they performed for the Elector Maximilian Joseph III at his palace. Later that same year the family made a trip to the city of Vienna. Here Nannerl and Wolferl, as they were nicknamed, delighted the Emperor and Empress with spectacular performances. The concerts took place in the beautiful palace of Schönbrunn, with its hundreds of rooms, its gardens and ponds. For four weeks they were frequent visitors, playing with the royal children as well as entertaining the family and their guests.

Once, after the six-year-old Wolfgang slipped on the polished floor, the seven-year-old Marie Antoinette helped him to his feet. "When I grow up I will marry you," he told her gratefully. This, alas, was not to be. She married the king of France.

From the Empress, the children received costumes made for the Archduke Maximilian and one of the archduchesses. These were fancy outfits of the finest materials. The children wore them with pride and had their portraits painted in them. The young Mozart looked especially regal wearing his powdered wig and carrying a sword.

While in Vienna, Wolferl came down with scarlet fever, and the family had to remain in quarantine for four weeks. His name day occurred during his illness; the gift from his father turned out to be a music notebook of his own. Even the child prodigy did not jiggle a joggle over *this* selection.

The Mozart family finally returned to Salzburg in January over roads that were almost impassable. Somehow the old town lacked luster after the glitter and glamor of the city of Vienna.

After a few months at home, the Mozarts, accompanied by their nineteen-year-old servant Sebastian Winter, set forth once more. They planned to make their way to Paris, visiting the larger cities and courts en route. They hoped to astound the natives and make a million thalers-- more or less.

One of the first stops on this trip was Augsburg, Leopold's home town. A month before their arrival, a letter, an advance press notice, came out in the local newspaper. Written by someone who had heard the children perform in Vienna (perhaps Leopold himself), it read:

Just imagine a girl eleven years of age who can perform on the harpsichord or fortepiano the most difficult sonatas and concertos by the greatest masters, most accurately, readily and with an almost incredible ease, in the very best of taste. This alone cannot fail to fill many with astonishment. But we fall into utter amazement on seeing a boy aged six at the clavier and hear him, not by any means toy with sonatas, trios, and concertos, but play in a manly way, and improvise moreover for hours on end out of his own head, now *cantabile* now in chords, producing the best of ideas according to the taste of today; and even accompany at sight symphonies, arias and recitatives. . . . What is more I saw them cover the keyboard with a handkerchief; and he plays just as well on cloth as though he could see the keys. Furthermore, I saw and heard how, when he was made to listen in another room, they would give him notes, now high, now low, not only on the pianoforte but on every other instrument as well, and he came out with a letter or the name of the note in an instant. Indeed, on hearing a bell toll or a clock, even a pocket watch, strike, he was able at the same moment to name the note of the bell or timepiece. I was also present in person when a clavier player on several occasions played a bar of melody for him, which he then repeated and had to fit a bass to of his own; and every time he carried this out so beautifully, accurately and well that everybody was astounded.

The children amazed their audiences wherever they performed. They made numerous stops along the route, sometimes in a monastery or a church where Wolferl would try out the organ, standing on the pedals in order to reach them. In Heidelberg, the boy so impressed the dean of the Cathedral with his organ playing that this dignitary had a description of the event inscribed on the organ console. They put on concerts in various courts and inns, and they listened to the famous Mannheim orchestra.

At Mainz they left their heavy luggage and took the market boat to Frankfurt. Here Leopold scratched his name and the date on the windowpane of the house where they stayed. A fourteen-year-old boy who attended one of the Frankfurt concerts became a famous poet. Years afterwards, Goethe still remembered hearing "the little man with the wig and the sword."

The young artists gave concerts in Coblenz, Bonn, Liége, Cologne, and Brussels. On November 18, they arrived in Paris. They spent Christmas Eve at the magnificent palace of Versailles with its high ceilings, spacious rooms, and colorful gardens. Here they played for King Louis XV, the Queen, and Madame de Pompadour. On New Year's Day, they were invited to watch the king and his family dine in state. The room was damp and cold. Wolferl stood in back of the queen, who fed him bits of food from her plate. She talked to him in German, "which," he said, "she speaks as well as we do."

In Paris, the Mozarts were befriended by a prominent journalist named Grimm. This gentleman, who later became a baron, was called the "musk bear," because he used so much powder and perfume. He publicized their concerts in his journal and, for the first one, sold 320 tickets. He also supplied the "wax lights"--60 large candles.

In addition to giving concerts with his sister, Wolfgang wrote two sonatas which he dedicated to one of the king's daughters. Leopold reported to his landlord in Salzburg, "The people are all crazy about my children."

In April, they left for Calais, where they hired a boat to take them to Dover, as the packet boat was already full when they arrived at the port. They all heaved a sigh of relief after they had safely crossed the English Channel.

In London, they checked in at the home of a barber, John Cousins, "hair cutter in Cecil Court, St. Martins Lane." Almost immediately, everyone sallied forth on a shopping spree. They bought hats for Nannerl and her mother, and dress clothes for Wolferl.

While in England, the children performed many times for the king and queen, giving several concerts. One took place in Hickford's Great Room: "a Grand Concert of Vocal and Instrumental Music." Performing were three singers, a violinist, a cellist, and a flutist, in addition to Wolfgang, who played a concerto on the harpsichord.

The boy took voice lessons from one of his new friends, a singer. When his father became ill, Wolfgang was unable to practice. He spent his time composing six sonatas for the harpsichord, dedicating them to Queen Charlotte who, according to Haydn, "played quite well for a queen."

After more than a year had passed, the Mozarts returned to the Continent, visiting Rotterdam, the Hague, Amsterdam, Brussels, Paris, Geneva, and Zurich. On the thirtieth of November 1766, the weary wanderers once more climbed the three flights of stairs to their apartment in Salzburg. They had been away from home over three years. Their trunks contained a potpourri of gifts: 9 pocket watches, 12 gold snuff boxes, gold rings set with precious stones, necklaces, earrings, bottle holders, toothpick boxes, writing tablets, knives with gold blades, and many other treasures. But the only fortune they had made was one of magnificent memories.

3. MOZART: *The Pianist*

Back home in Salzburg, Wolfgang kept busy composing and playing for court festivities. At the age of thirteen, he became Konzertmeister at the court and wrote canons, suites, concertos, string quartets, symphonies, and operas. On Sundays, the Mozarts and their friends amused themselves in a game of bowls, weather permitting.

The young musician made trips to Vienna and Munich--and to Italy, where he took counterpoint lessons from Padre Martini. While in Rome, he listened to a Holy Week presentation of Allegri's *Miserere.* This music was regarded as being too sacred to be taken from the chapel, but the fourteen-year-old returned to his room and wrote out the entire work from memory. On Good Friday, manuscript in hand, he went again to church and made the few necessary corrections as the choir repeated its performance.

In the Fall of 1777, Wolfgang set out with his mother on another long tour that eventually took him to Paris. (His father had been unable to obtain leave from his position as Vice-Kapellmeister.) After a short stop in Munich, where he tried unsuccessfully to obtain some sort of appointment, Wolfgang and his mother left for Augsburg. Here they stayed with Leopold's brother, and the young man found a pal in his cousin, whom he called "das Bäsle." Like him, she was fun-loving and jolly.

He enjoyed a visit to the piano shop of Johann Andreas Stein and wrote his father describing and praising this man's fortepianos. In a later letter he commented on the playing of Stein's eight-year-old daughter, Maria Anna: "Anyone who sees and hears her play and can keep from laughing must, like her father, be made of stone. [As he so often did, Mozart was playing with words, for 'Stein' in German means 'stone.'] For instead of sitting in the middle of the clavier, she sits right up opposite the treble, as it gives her more chance of flopping about and making grimaces. She rolls her eyes and smirks. When a passage is repeated, she plays it more slowly the second time. If it has to be played a third time, then she plays it even more slowly. When a passage is being played, the arm must be raised as high as possible, and according as the notes in the passage are stressed, the arm, not the fingers must do this, and that too with great emphasis and clumsy manner. But the best joke of all is that when she comes to a passage that ought to flow like oil and which necessitates a change of finger, she does not bother her head about it, but when the moment arrives she just leaves out the notes, raises her hand and starts off again quite comfortably, a method by which she is much more likely to strike a wrong note."

Wolfgang gave a few concerts in Augsburg, playing both the violin and the clavier. Of a performance in the local monastery he wrote that the orchestra there, bad though it might be, was better than the town orchestra. He had previously reported that this one was "enough to give one a fit."

When they reached Mannheim, Wolfgang found a superior orchestra. He became friendly with many of its members, some of whom remembered his visit when he was a boy. Much as a child picks flowers to present to those he likes, Mozart wrote music for many of the musicians: flute, oboe, clarinet, and violin concertos. Rosa Cannabich, the conductor's daughter, studied piano with him, so he composed music for her, also. He gave lessons in composition in return for his mother's meals. He himself dined regularly at the home of his friend who played the flute, Herr Wendling.

In Mannheim, he met a young opera singer--she was only fifteen--and fell in love with her. He thought Aloysia Weber sang his music better than anyone he had ever heard. Because of her, he tried especially hard to find a suitable position. Despite the combined efforts of his musical buddies, his attempts were unsuccessful. But, being in love, he found all sorts of excuses for dilly-dallying in Mannheim.

His father's frantic fuming finally forced him to make arrangements to start out for Paris. Early in March, mother and son climbed into a carriage and once more resigned themselves to the ordeal of traveling. And what an ordeal it turned out to be! Like many roads in the early spring, the streets were sometimes muddy, sometimes icy, but always bumpy. The journey dragged on for ten whole days. When at long last they reached their destination, Wolfgang complained, "Never in my life have I endured such tedium."

Paris did not seem the glamorous city Mozart had remembered from his childhood. The streets were dirty and muddy. They could not find pleasant rooms, at least not any that were large enough to take Wolfgang's clavier. At home they had been used to a spacious apartment and food that was not as highly seasoned as that the French served.

Actually, Paris was not as impressed with a twenty-two-year-old virtuoso as it had been with a child prodigy. But young Mozart did some playing, some composing, and some teaching; and he listened to lots of music. One of the highlights was an unexpected meeting with his old friend, Mr. John Bach, who happened to be in town on business. Wolfgang turned down an offer of a position as organist at Versailles because of the low salary and isolated location. He received no other offers.

Finally, real tragedy entered his life. His mother became seriously ill and died within two weeks' time, leaving him alone in a city that failed to properly recognize his superior talent. Even Baron Grimm tired of futile attempts to find him a permanent position and purchased the ticket that started the slow, wormlike crawl back to Salzburg.

Mozart gave concerts in Strasbourg, and he lingered in Mannheim. Finally he arrived at the home of the Webers, who had moved to Munich. Here he met with further disappointment, for he discovered that Aloysia no longer took an interest in him. He stayed on anyway, writing music for her and enjoying the orchestra and his Mannheim friends now established in Munich.

After his father prevailed upon him to return to Salzburg, Wolfgang received an appointment as Court Organist. But he never felt content in his home town. When he had a falling-out with the Archbishop while they were both in Vienna, he seized the opportunity and remained there. Mozart rented a room with the Webers, who had moved again when Aloysia obtained an appointment at the

National Theatre in Vienna. He fell in love once more--with Constanza, a younger sister of Aloysia's. This time his love was returned, and they were married.

For a while, the two love birds seemed to perch on a swing that reached almost to the sky. Both were easy going, happy-go-lucky individuals. When they had money, they splurged on expensive clothes, a billiard table, bottles of wine, or parties. One affair--a sort of housewarming for their second apartment--began at six in the evening and finally broke up at seven in the morning. They had danced all night.

In 1784 Mozart acquired a fortepiano built by Anton Walther of Vienna. Over seven feet long, it had a range of about five octaves and a damper pedal for the foot instead of the customary knee control. At first the pianist and his new piano were in constant demand.

During his only visit to their home, Leopold wrote his daughter Marianne, "We never get to bed before one o'clock and I never get up before nine. We lunch at two or half past. . . . Every day there are concerts, and the whole time is given up to teaching, music, composing, etc. It's impossible for me to describe the rush and hustle. Since my arrival [he had been there four or five days] your brother's fortepiano has been taken at least a dozen times to the theatre or to some other house."

On the day after Leopold arrived, Wolfgang gave the first of six subscription concerts. About 150 signed up in advance for these happenings. For each, he composed one or two new concertos as well as other instrumental numbers. He wrote arias for various singers such as Aloysia Weber Lang. Sometimes he stayed up until dawn the night before one of these concerts. Occasionally he had no time to write out his own part, so he accompanied from memory. These were the "happy times" which all too soon came to a screeching halt.

As the years passed, the problems increased. Constanza had many babies, and most of them died as infants. There were endless doctor's bills and endless funeral bills. The couple moved twelve times in nine years. They fell deeper and deeper into debt. By 1787, Mozart could no longer find subscribers for his concerts, and they were discontinued.

The trials of his personal life never seemed to dam up the flood of music that poured from his happy-talking pen. He turned his attention to writing operas. *The Marriage of Figaro* became especially popular in Prague, where he found that "nothing is played, sung, or whistled but *Figaro*." His opera *Don Giovanni* also met with loud applause there. One of his last operas, *The Magic Flute*, he composed in a little summer house that can now be seen in the Mozarteum garden in Salzburg.

From the reminiscences of a tenor who sang in some of the operas, we have a word picture of the composer. "He was a remarkably small man, very thin and pale, with a profusion of fine hair, of which he was rather vain. He always received me with kindness and hospitality. He was remarkably fond of punch. He was also fond of billiards and had an excellent billiard table in his house. Many and many a game have I played with him, but always came off second best. He was kindhearted and always ready to oblige, but so very particular when he played that if the slightest noise was made, he instantly left off."

Mozart was not quite 36 years old when he died, leaving over 600 finished compositions. They included nearly 50 symphonies and 30 piano concertos. At the time of his death, he was working on a requiem, which had to be completed by his favorite pupil.

Wolfgang Amadeus Mozart was given a third-class funeral and buried in an unmarked pauper's grave. The music he left to the world is strictly first-class. It is his tallest monument and one that everyone can enjoy.

Another memorial is the one offered by Mozart's home town. Every summer, the city of Salzburg comes alive with festivities. People swarm to his birthplace with its quaint kitchen and antique instruments such as the Walther fortepiano. Or they saunter along the Getreidegasse under the delicate wrought-iron shop signs. They peer into the many beautiful churches and the Cathedral, or they climb to the fortress and admire the view.

Music is everywhere. It floats from the practice rooms of the Mozarteum, from the Glockenspiel tower, or from the "Horn Work" of the old fort. It floods the opera and concert hall stages, and even the flowers in the Mirabell Gardens and all the fountains of the city seem to join in the celebration.

Mirabell Gardens with fortress in background. Salzburg, Austria

4. *MUZIO CLEMENTI*

Early in 1781, a distinguished visitor arrived in Vienna. Muzio Clementi enjoyed the reputation of a piano virtuoso. The Emperor decided to arrange a competition between this talented stranger and Austria's greatest pianist, Wolfgang Amadeus Mozart. Such a contest, a popular happening in the eighteenth century, always sparked interest among those fortunate enough to be present.

Clementi describes his arrival at the palace: "On entering the music room I beheld an individual whose elegant attire led me to mistake him for an imperial *valet-de-chambre*. But we had no sooner entered into conversation than it turned on musical topics, and we soon recognized each other, with sincere pleasure, brother artists--Mozart and Clementi."

The program opened with two solos by Clementi: his Sonata in B-flat (Op. 47, No. 2) and an improvised toccata in which he showed off his specialty: rapid passages in thirds and double notes. He used a Broadwood piano. Mozart had borrowed a Stein piano from Countess Thun, a generous patron of music and a friend of his. On this he improvised a prelude and set of variations. Then each sight-read some sonatas that had been brought by the Grand Duchess. Mozart played the allegros, and Clementi the adagios and rondos. Finally they were asked to take a theme from one of these sonatas and develop it on two pianos. For this feat, the Emperor asked Mozart to use the palace piano, even though, as Wolfgang later reported, "It was out of tune and had three keys that stuck."

Neither pianist won first prize. The Emperor declared a tie, for each excelled in his own way. Clementi may have possessed the better technique. Mozart called him a "mere mechanic," saying, "His star passages

are thirds. Apart from that he had not a farthing's worth of feeling."
Clementi--more charitable--praised Mozart's singing tone and good taste.
In later years, he worked on a singing legato of his own, aided by technical
improvement made in the English pianos.

Muzio Clementi was at least four years older than Wolfgang Mozart.
He was born in Rome, and his father was a silversmith who made art
objects for the wealthier Italian churches. The child showed unusual talent
for music when very young and received his first instruction at seven, first
from a choir master and then from an organist. According to his father, he
was only nine years old when he won a competition for the position of
organist in one of the Roman churches.

When Muzio was fourteen, he played for an Englishman who,
impressed by his ability, offered to take him to England and supervise his
training. The boy spent seven years in Peter Beckford's country house in
Dorsetshire, where he practiced the harpsichord eight hours a day and
composed. In his spare time, he took advantage of his patron's magnificent
library, becoming a scholar with many interests. These ranged from Latin
literature to astronomy and included several languages.

After moving to London, Clementi fell under John Bach's magic spell.
He published his first keyboard sonatas and started to appear in concerts.
He taught harpsichord and piano, and his fee averaged five dollars per
lesson, unusually high for the period. He served as orchestral conductor
of the Italian opera at the king's theatre for a few years before going to
Paris in 1780. Here Clementi gave concerts and played for Marie
Antoinette.

At the time of the contest with Mozart in Vienna, Clementi was on a
tour that included Paris, Strasbourg, and Munich. Back in London in
March of 1784, he took part in the first two-piano recital on record. The
second pianist was Clementi's thirteen-year-old pupil, Johann Baptist
Cramer. Nicknamed "Glorious John," this boy later became famous not
only for his piano playing--Beethoven called him "the only good pianist of
his time"--but for his use of snuff. He was a problem to all housekeepers,
who had to clean up spilled snuff after every visit. Even more disturbing,
his snuff sometimes clogged the action of the piano keys.

Another pupil to become famous as pianist and composer was John
Field. After Clementi involved himself in the music publishing business

and in the manufacturing of pianos, he no longer took time to practice. He hired Field to demonstrate his pianos. Neither too well-clothed nor too well-fed, Field worked long hours at practicing and selling. Finally, Clementi took him to Paris, Vienna, and to Russia, where his concerts met with glowing success.

When London's Philharmonic Society was founded in 1813, Clementi became its first conductor. He wrote symphonies for the concerts that, as the *Morning Chronicle* reported, "lost nothing by comparison though in the company of Haydn, Mozart and Beethoven." Clementi wrote much of his music for piano students. There were 64 sonatas and 100 technical studies called *Gradus ad Parnassum* (steps to Mount Parnassus, a mythological goal of all artists). This particular work he called his last "Will and Testament."

Clementi's *Introduction to the Art of Playing on the Piano Forte* was one of the first so-called "tutors" to include the music of well-known composers. The book presents many of Clementi's rules and principles, including one that "all unnecessary motion [of hand and arm] must be avoided." To achieve this, he had his students practice with coins on the backs of their hands.

Clementi's life was not all rippling arpeggios--there were a few dissonant chords. When he tried to elope with a sixteen-year-old pupil, her father intervened. His first wife died a few days after giving birth to a son. He lost money in a firm that went bankrupt. He had to sell some snuff boxes and jewelry after his piano factory, which was not adequately insured, burned.

Having once been considered the foremost virtuoso pianist, Clementi did not want to be heard when out of practice. After agreeing to play for the Empress in Vienna, he covered the piano in a quilt and barricaded himself in a room with mattress pads against the door. Then he practiced.

For many years, Clementi used the same excuse for refusing to play when asked. He said his hand was stiff from a fall from a sled in Russia. But there were still occasions that inspired him to sit down at the piano. The pianist Moscheles, who called Clementi one of the "most vigorous old fellows" he ever saw, reported that at a dinner given in his honor, the 76-year-old musician improvised "with the fire and brilliance of youth." His eyes sparkled and the rafters rang with thunderous applause.

Clementi died a wealthy man at the age of 80. Some said he had been a miser. He is buried in Westminster Abbey, and the inscription on his tombstone calls him "The Father of the Pianoforte."

MUZIO CLEMENTI

called

The Father of the Pianoforte

His fame as a musician
and Composer
Acknowledged Throughout Europe
Procured Him the Honour
of a Public Interment
in this Cloister

Born at Rome 1752
Died at Evesham 1832

(Inscription on Clementi's tombstone, Westminster Abbey)

5. *LUDWIG VAN BEETHOVEN: Introduction (Bonn)*

While visiting Vienna in 1807, Clementi often dined with a pupil at an inn called "The Swan." Here he frequently observed the famous Ludwig Van Beethoven also dining with a pupil. But since each felt the other should make the first move, they never spoke. Years later they did get together, and Beethoven granted Clementi the right to publish his music in England. Elated by this triumph, Clementi reported to his partner, "I have at last made a conquest of the haughty beauty, Beethoven."

Ludwig was born on December 16, 1770 in the attic of a small house in Bonn, Germany. In this town, his grandfather, for whom Ludwig was named, had started his career as a bass singer in the court choir. Eventually he became its leader, or Kapellmeister. Ludwig's father sang soprano, contralto, and then tenor in the same choir. He also taught clavier and singing and was his son's first teacher. Lessons began for Ludwig at an early age--probably four --and the lad had to practice long hours on both the piano and violin.

When he was seven, Ludwig appeared in a concert. The announcement read:

> Today, March 26, 1778, in the musical concert-room in the Sternengass the Electoral Court Tenorist, BEETHOVEN will have the honor to present two of his scholars; namely, Mdlle. Averdonck, Court Contraltist, and his little son of six years. The former will have the honor to contribute various beautiful arias, the latter various clavier concertos and trios,

in which he flatters himself that he will give complete enjoyment to all ladies and gentlemen, the more since both have had the honor of playing to the greatest delight of the entire Court.
Beginning at five o'clock in the evening.

At about the age of nine, "Luis" began to study with other teachers. He became an assistant organist in the Franciscan Cloister. In the Cloister of the Minorites, he played for the 6 a.m. Mass. His fame spread outside Bonn when he and his mother took the boat down the Rhine to Holland. All his relatives expressed amazement upon hearing him play.

Beethoven studied piano, organ, theory, and composition with Neefe, the court organist. When only twelve, he became cembalist of the court orchestra, acquiring valuable experience in playing the harpsichord and conducting from an orchestral score. At the age of thirteen he was appointed organist to the court and earned a small salary. He also tried his hand at composing, writing three pianoforte sonatas. According to a neighbor, he could be seen walking along the street wearing a "sea-green tailcoat, short green trousers with buckles, silk stockings, and a white silk waistcoat decorated with floral motif. He wore his hair in curls with a pigtail behind and carried an opera hat and a sword complete with belt."

In 1784, the Archduke Maximilian became Elector of the Court of Bonn. He loved music and the theatre, and founded a national theatre company. Ludwig played the viola in the theatre orchestra, becoming familiar with the operatic repertoire of the day.

He worked hard but managed to manufacture his own brand of fun. On one occasion, he accompanied a singer who gave permission for improvisation in the organ accompaniment. Ludwig's imagination wandered so far afield that the soloist couldn't find the closing cadence. This amused the Elector, but he "forbade such clever tricks in the future."

In 1787, Ludwig visited Vienna and played for Mozart. After hearing him improvise, Wolfgang is reported to have said, "Keep your eyes on him; some day he will give the world something to talk about."

Beethoven may also have had a few lessons with Mozart before being called back to Bonn because of his mother's serious illness. When she died, he said he had lost his "best friend." Not long after, his baby sister died. At the age of sixteen, he became responsible for two younger brothers and an alcoholic father, who proved more of a problem than a help to him.

At about this time, Eleanore Breuning, a wealthy widow, engaged Beethoven to teach her fifteen-year-old daughter and ten-year-old son. Ludwig spent much of his free time with this educated and scholarly family, who introduced him to forms of culture other than music. Poetry and the ancient Greek classics, especially Homer and Plutarch, were read in the original Greek under the guidance of a tutor. Ludwig and Eleanore Breuning--and the man she married, Dr. Wegeler--remained friends all their lives.

When the court orchestra made a two-month excursion up the Rhine and Main Rivers to Mergentheim, they played so well that one listener compared them to the Mannheim orchestra. They created a striking picture in their red and gold uniforms. Behind the scenes, Ludwig served the group as a kitchen boy. Eventually he worked his way from galley slave to star performer.

Beethoven played his recently published set of variations and distinguished himself with his improvisations and sight-reading. But the piano sometimes suffered. Anton Reicha, a friend who played the flute, told about turning pages of a Mozart concerto for him: "I was mostly occupied in wrenching the strings of the pianoforte which snapped, while the hammers struck among the broken strings. Beethoven insisted on finishing the concerto, and so back and forth I leapt, jerking out a string, disentangling a hammer, turning a page, and I worked harder than Beethoven."

Another friend, Count Waldstein, apparently presented him with a piano. The count may also have had a part in persuading the Elector to send the talented youth to Vienna to study with Haydn. In 1792, Beethoven left his family and friends, the beautiful Rhine valley and river he loved so much--"Our Father Rhine" he called it--and set out for Vienna.

He took with him an autograph album which he passed among his friends. One page included a quotation from Herder, which reads in translation:

Friendship, with that which is good,
Grows like the evening shadow
Till the setting sun of life.

Bonn, the 1st of November, 1792 Your true friend Eleanore Bruening

Ludwig in court dress (1786)
Silhouette by Neesen

6. BEETHOVEN: *Development and Finale (Vienna)*

In Vienna, Beethoven occupied himself with the details of getting settled in a strange city. He rented an attic room and sat down to list his needs in a memorandum book. Entries included: "wood, wig-maker, coffee, overcoat, boots, shoes, pianoforte-desk, seal, writing-desk, pianoforte money." He looked through the local newspaper for piano ads, and he wrote down the name and address of a dancing teacher. He had to plan carefully, for he'd received from the Elector only twenty-five ducats instead of the one hundred he had expected.

When the newcomer moved into rooms on the ground floor, he saved money in one way. An entry in the memorandum book reads, "It is not necessary to give the housekeeper more than 7 florins, the rooms are so close to the ground."

He soon saved in another way, for one of the tenants invited Beethoven to move into his apartment as a guest. This kind soul was none other that Prince Lichnowsky, a well-known patron of music who had been a friend and pupil of Mozart.

Every Friday morning, the prince hired a group of four or five musicians to come in to make music. They frequently performed Beethoven's works and sometimes made suggestions regarding them. On one occasion, when they were playing a few numbers by another Viennese composer, the cellist lost his place. Beethoven stood up and, still playing his own part, proceeded to sing the cello part, which he couldn't have known from heart. This feat impressed Dr. Wegeler, who happened to be present. But the young genius tossed it off by saying that the cello part had to be as he had sung it, or the composer would have known nothing about writing music.

Upon arriving in Vienna, Beethoven began to study counterpoint and composition with "Papa Haydn," the famous Kapellmeister at Esterhazy. Haydn had praised one of Beethoven's cantatas he'd seen when visiting Bonn. Soon Beethoven became dissatisfied with his lessons and started to study secretly with Johann Schenk. But he remained on friendly terms with his original teacher. According to his memorandum book, he occasionally spent a few kreutzers for coffee or chocolate "für Haydn und mich." When Haydn left for England, his pupil transferred to Albrechtsberger, Vienna's most famous counterpoint teacher.

Because of his talent, it did not take long for Beethoven to win his way into the hearts of the nobility. His playing of J.S. Bach's music may have provided the opening wedge to Baron Van Swieten's circle of musicians. After one of his musicales, Van Swieten "detained Beethoven and persuaded him to add a few fugues by Sebastian Bach as an evening blessing." That the two were good friends is shown by the fact that the pianist received an invitation to a pajama party in the baron's house. It read:

> To Herr Beethoven in Alstergasse, No. 45, with the Prince Lichnowsky: If there is nothing to hinder next Wednesday I should be glad to see you at my home at half past 8 with your nightcap in your bag. Give me an immediate answer.
>
> Swieten

While Beethoven soon became favorite in the private salons, he did not play in public in Vienna until 1795. He then appeared as pianist and composer at the annual concerts for the benefit of widows and orphans of fellow musicians. On March 29, he played a concerto he had written for piano and orchestra. The following night, he improvised, and on the 31st, he performed a Mozart concerto. The Viennese were overwhelmed by his "fiery expression."

They were also carried away by his ability to improvise. One of Ludwig's first acquaintances was a virtuoso pianist and composer, the Abbé Joseph Gelinek. Someone arranged a contest between them. The Abbé bragged that he would soon take care of the upstart. After the concert, he adopted a new attitude, saying, ". . . he is no man; he's a devil. He will play me and all of us to death. And how he improvises!"

Carl Czerny wrote, "Nobody equalled him in the rapidity of his scales, double trills, skips, etc.--not even Hummel. His bearing while playing was masterfully quiet, noble and beautiful, without the slightest grimace (only bent forward low, as his deafness grew upon him); his fingers were very powerful, not long, and broadened at the tips by much playing, for he told me very often indeed that he generally had to practice until after midnight in his youth."

In 1796, Beethoven made trips to Prague, Berlin, Pressburg, and Budapest. In Berlin he played at the court of King Frederick William II, being rewarded with a gold snuffbox filled with money. He took much pride in this and boasted that, "It was not an ordinary snuffbox, but such an one as it might have been customary to give an ambassador."

Shortly after the turn of the century, Beethoven gave the first public concert in Vienna for his own benefit. The program began at 6:30 p.m. It consisted of improvisations, a symphony by Mozart, arias, one of his own concertos, and one of his own symphonies.

In his teaching, Beethoven, like Clementi, insisted on legato playing. He called Mozart's detached style "finger dancing" or "manual air-sawing." He was particular about hand position, scales in all keys, and use of the thumb. He had several pupils among the nobility, and many of them were women. One, a countess, lived nearby. He once arrived for her lesson wearing morning gown, slippers, and a tasseled cap. Czerny, who studied with him for three years, would often be handed a freshly composed sonata to sightread.

Many of his works were dedicated to pupils. In return for one such dedication he received a horse, which he rode for a few days and then forgot. He didn't even remember to feed it. His servant took care of this detail, at the same time making some money on the side by renting out the animal. Since he did not wish to call attention to this horseplay, he held back the bills for feed. Finally he turned them in. Beethoven, for once in his life, appeared completely dumfounded.

Finale

Some time around 1798, Beethoven began to be troubled by ringing in his ears. He had never been too well, and worry over losing his hearing added to his other health problems. For a while he avoided his friends rather than face the embarrassment of telling them of his deafness. He did seek the advice of some of Vienna's most famous doctors. One suggested cold baths; another prescribed tepid baths in the Danube and applied to both arms an ointment made from the seed of a daphne plant. A priest dropped fluid in his ear every day, which might have helped eventually, but this practice proved too bothersome for the busy musician.

By 1815, Beethoven communicated almost entirely in writing. His days of conducting or playing in public were about over. Composing became the only musical activity left to him. He could at least hear his creations with the ear of his mind. He compared the tones that roared and stormed about him to the moods that a poet transforms into verse.

Many of his themes occurred to him while walking around Vienna or in one of the places in the country where he spent his summers. He would jot down the theme on a piece of manuscript paper he always had with him. Later he transferred it to a sketchbook where it could be molded and developed. He often worked on more than one composition at a time.

Much of Beethoven's music was favorably received during his lifetime, and it was considered as important as the music of Mozart and Haydn. He wrote nine symphonies, the last containing a final chorus that celebrates joy. In addition, there were 32 piano sonatas, variations for piano, 5 piano concertos, 1 violin concerto, a triple concerto for piano, violin, and cello, the opera *Fidelio*, 2 masses, a cantata, an oratorio, dozens of songs, 16 string quartets, a number of smaller works for piano solo, and chamber music for a variety of instruments. Some of his orchestral music he arranged for piano as well.

That he accomplished so much seems miraculous. His living quarters --which he changed frequently--invariably resembled a disaster area. And the poor man often wasted hours searching for mysteriously misplaced material among the piles of paper and manuscripts. He never married, despite the fact that being in love was practically a perpetual state for him. The objects of his affection were usually musicians, often his pupils. Many were of noble birth, countesses or baronesses, and almost all were young and beautiful.

When he kept house, he suffered the ordeal of engaging and managing servants who came and went with astonishing regularity. Some of his experiences with the hired help are recorded in notes to a neighbor, Nanette Streicher, who tried to help him with his housekeeping problems. (She was the Maria Anna Stein of Augsburg, who had amused Mozart with her gyrations at the piano. When she married, she and her husband and brother moved to Vienna, where they built and sold pianos.)

In one note, Beethoven reports that a maid seemed to have improved after the first of January. "I wished her a 'Happy New Year' by throwing half a dozen books at her head," he boasted. Another maid, Baberl, had fared no better on a different occasion. He relates that when "they both resumed their devilish tricks, I made short work of them and threw the heavy chair beside my bed at B."

He took time for friendship, placing it high on his priority list. Many of his acquaintances spent only part of their lives in Vienna, some being touring musicians who happened to visit the city. Beethoven could be hard to get along with, and sometimes his best friends became his worst enemies, at least temporarily.

One friendship began at an informal get-together. A violinist playing a solo was startled to discover that the man who had stepped forward to turn his pages was the great Beethoven himself. After their future meetings, they walked each other home, as children sometimes do.

Correspondence with publishers consumed much of the composer's time. That he possessed a sense of humor is revealed in his letters to Steiner, a Vienna publisher. In an imaginary military organization, Beethoven was the

Generalissimo; Steiner was the Lieutenant General; and his partner, Haslinger, the Adjunct. The copyist and proofreader, Diabelli, was the Provost Marshal, with Steiner's workshop as the headquarters. Too many errors resulted in a court martial. Numerous letters had to be written to numerous publishers, giving instructions for correcting the many mistakes and setting fees for each composition.

Beethoven fared much better that Mozart, but there were still times when he found himself in financial difficulties. When one of his brothers died, he became his nephew's guardian. In his new role, he exchanged time and money for heartache and aggravation, despite the fact that he loved children and tried to do what he thought best for his nephew.

In one letter, Beethoven wrote, "In order to gain some leisure for the great work, I must always scrawl a good deal beforehand for money, so that I can keep alive while I am composing the great work." Another letter reads: "In order to keep myself alive I had to finish off several potboilers." At one time, he received a regular salary from three of Vienna's wealthy citizens, but this arrangement lasted only a short while.

Several manufacturers sent him pianos as gifts. Equally hard on all of them, Beethoven was said to have broken more pianos than anyone else had broken in Vienna. His very favorite piano was the grand sent to him in 1818 by England's John Broadwood & Sons. It had a range of over six octaves and thrilled him beyond words--an answer to his prayer for a piano that was more than a harp. He banged away on it, trying to hear some slight sound. Soon it became a tangle of wires. His tuner reported that, "The upper registers were mute, and the broken strings in a tangle, like a thorn bush whipped by a storm." When he tried to play softly, he frequently came up with no sound at all. One writer commented, "The instrument is actually as dumb as the musician is deaf."

Beethoven loved nature in all its outbursts of glory: flowers, clouds, trees! "No one on earth can love the country as much as I," he wrote. Later: "I love a tree more than a man." In speaking of his compositions, he said that "Compared with the works of the Highest, everything is small."

On March 26, 1827, Vienna was dealt a violent snowstorm accompanied by loud claps of thunder. Appropriately enough, this powerful, exciting giant of music--bedridden for four months--made his exit from the world at the height of this fortissimo spectacle of nature.

Beethoven's Broadwood piano (1817)
Courtesy of Magyar Nemzeto Muzeum (Budapest, Hungary)

7.   HUMMEL, CZERNY, and MOSCHELES

Vienna could boast of three other gifted pianists who spent part of their lives in its realm and who knew Beethoven. One of these was Johann Nepomuk Hummel. Born in Bohemia in 1778, he began study with Mozart at the age of seven and lived with him for two years. He then went to London where Clementi gave him lessons. Later he returned to Vienna for instruction from Haydn. When still a young man, Hummel succeeded Haydn as Kapellmeister to Prince Esterhazy, eventually being relieved of this position for supposed "neglect of duty."

The pianist moved to Vienna and proceeded to score musical touchdowns with his brilliant playing. Soon, the city's music lovers divided themselves into two teams. Hummel's supporters proclaimed Beethoven's playing noisy and overpedaled. Beethoven's cheerleaders called Hummel's style "monotonous as a hurdy-gurdy," and they added that his fingers reminded them of spiders.

Hummel adorned most of these fingers with valuable diamond rings, complementing this elegance with somewhat sloppy attire. His face was pitted by smallpox, and he could never have won a beauty contest. In later years, he grew really roly-poly and had to have a place carved out of his dining tables at home and at court to accommodate his protuberance.

When Hummel played the piano, he huffed and puffed and mopped his brow. His improvisations were exciting, and his compositions were popular in his day. Considered an authority on music, he wrote many books concerning the art of playing the piano.

*   *   *

One of the first to jump on Hummel's bandwagon was Carl Czerny. He immediately arranged for lessons after hearing Hummel play. Czerny, a native of Vienna, was born the year that Mozart died. His father presided as his first teacher. At the age of ten, the child began to study with Beethoven, who showed his approval a few years later with written endorsement. It mentioned his "extraordinary progress on the pianoforte" and his "astonishing memory." Beethoven also selected Czerny as his nephew's piano teacher.

By the time he reached sixteen years of age, Czerny had established himself as a teacher. Sometimes he gave as many as twelve lessons a day, taking only gifted or advanced students. He worked out all kinds of exciting exercises for his pupils. Some say he must have hated children, but his technical studies still contribute to the blossoming of many a budding pianist.

Czerny's *Complete Theoretical and Practical Pianoforte School* included instruction for selecting, tuning, and restringing a piano. He wrote his autobiography and edited Bach's keyboard works and 200 Scarlatti sonatas. The number of his own compositions exceeded one thousand. It is said that he kept four or five music stands set up and, skullcap on his head, rushed from one to another. By composing a page here and a page there, he wasted no time waiting for ink to dry.

An only child who never married, Czerny loved cats. Usually seven or eight of them prowled about the house or slept in the chairs. He spent many hours hunting up good homes for the kittens.

Czerny's parents held recitals for his students every Sunday in their home. He himself seldom played in public. He disliked traveling and let the world come up to *his* door. His two most famous pupils were Franz Liszt and Theodor Leschetizky.

When he died, Carl Czerny left a considerable amount of money to charities and to the Vienna Conservatory.

*   *   *

Ignaz Moscheles was born in Prague in 1794. At the age of ten, he could play Beethoven's "Sonata Pathétique" from memory. He composed cadenzas for Beethoven's piano concertos and arranged his opera *Fidelio* for piano. In addition, he translated into English a biography of Beethoven.

Moscheles toured as a concert pianist. When he returned to Vienna, he borrowed his famous friend's Broadwood piano for one of his concerts. After his marriage, he lived in England and became active as a concert artist, conductor, and teacher.

One year, according to his diary, he gave 1,457 lessons. His fee was $10.50 per hour. Themes for composition often occurred to him while he walked from one pupil's house to another's. He jotted them down on a scrap of paper and then worked them out at home in the evening. The following day, his wife sat down at the piano and practiced what he had written.

Moscheles started out as a real virtuoso of the Classic School. He played quietly, using no wrist or arm motion and little pedaling. Early in his career he composed a showy set of variations called *Alexander's March*. As is the case with so many of today's singers who are often asked to sing the popular songs with which they are associated, Moscheles received requests to perform *Alexander's March* wherever he appeared. His later compositions exhibited more musicianship, and he became more scholarly. He then played only the best music, helping to upgrade the public taste. Some of his etudes --more musically imaginative than Czerny's--may interest today's advanced students.

Moscheles lived to be 76 years old, witnessing changes in both the piano and the music written for it. He adjusted rather slowly to what poured from the pens of younger composers but was one of the first to recognize the genius of Robert Schumann. "The proper ground for finger gymnastics," he wrote, "is to be found in Thalberg's latest compositions, but for soul give me Schumann." Once he had heard Chopin play his own compositions, he became a fan of his, also.

One of his best friends, Felix Mendelssohn, studied with him as a teenager. After Mendelssohn founded a Conservatory in Leipzig, he invited his former teacher to join the faculty. Moscheles taught there for twenty years, loved by all who knew him well.

The English called him "The Prince of Pianists."

Ignaz Moscheles (1794-1870)

8. *FELIX MENDELSSOHN*

As a child, Felix Mendelssohn seemed to live under a magic spell. The wand may have been the name "Felix," which means "happy" in Latin. Or the enchantment may have been conjured up by his background: his grandfather was a prominent philosopher, his father a banker, and his mother a talented musician who spoke several languages. Born in Hamburg, Germany, in 1809, Felix moved with his family to a ten-acre estate in Berlin when he was two years old.

The house resembled a miniature palace and the grounds a city park. The children--two boys and two girls--put on masks and dashed about, they climbed on roofs and meowed like cats, and they produced plays and operettas.

Both Felix and his older sister Fanny took their first piano lessons from their mother. Later, Felix studied with a pupil of Clementi and with the famous Moscheles. At the age of eight, he could play Beethoven symphonies on the piano from memory. When ten years old, Felix joined singing classes at the Singakademie. Here, among the grown-ups, he is pictured with hands in his pockets, tossing his long brown curls from side to side as he shifted from one foot to the other.

With the director of the Singakademie, Carl Friedrich Zelter, Felix studied harmony, counterpoint and composition. Sometimes standing on a chair to conduct, he presented many of his compositions at the famous Sunday musicales held in the garden pavilion of his home. It seated several hundred guests. These included scientists, painters, writers, and musicians from out of town as well as local celebrities.

The garden provided an ideal spot for composing, and Felix concocted his *Midsummer Night's Dream* overture here when seventeen. But his life as a teenager consisted of much more than writing music in a garden and playing the piano. He played the violin, viola, and cello, and studied Greek in addition to the routine subjects. With two of his friends he edited an informal, handwritten newspaper called *The Garden Times* in summer and *The Snow and Tea Times* in winter. Famous guests sometimes offered contributions.

Athletically inclined, Felix had a tutor in gymnastics. He swam well and loved to dance. At the regular family dances he took on his sisters' friends one after another. Someone said he danced "like a cultivated gale." Once, while walking along the street, he startled the man who walked just ahead by leaping onto his back.

Felix perpetrated another of his pranks while waiting to play for Goethe: he took a bellows from the fireplace and disrupted a young lady's hairdo with it. Sometimes his friends could get even with the prankster. Although his motor purred merrily, merrily most of the time, Felix felt compelled to lie down whenever he saw a sofa or a couch. Some called this his "ready fatigability." Once, when he fell fast asleep, his sister Rebecca sewed his coat to the couch.

Mendelssohn studied at the University of Berlin, doing well in all his subjects. At the age of twenty, he made the first of ten trips to England. As soon as he saw London, he fell in love with the city. Its excitement and variety left him "confused and topsy-turvy." He liked the English roast beef and rice pudding. He enjoyed sketching the scenery and flirting with the girls.

The Royal Philharmonic played his C-minor symphony and the *Midsummer Night's Dream* overture. The society made him an honorary member after he dedicated his symphony to them. With Moscheles, Mendelssohn played his two-piano concerto, writing home that they "had no end of fun." The English audiences responded to the man and his music with enthusiastic applause.

Upon his return to Germany, Felix visited Goethe at Weimar. He so impressed the poet with his playing and improvising that Goethe kept dreaming up excuses to keep him there, one of these being to have his portrait painted.

From Weimar, Mendelssohn went to Munich, Salzburg, Vienna, and then into Italy. Here he composed, made sketches of favorite scenes, and did some reading. During afternoons, the tourist wandered about admiring the paintings, sculptures, and architecture for which Italy is famous.

Like Mozart, Felix wrote interesting letters about what he saw and heard. He found the music inferior to that of Germany and England. The secular music he heard in Rome he described as "real cats' music," saying "it gives me a toothache." From Naples he wrote: "The first violinist all through the opera beats the four quarters of each bar on a tin candlestick, which is often more distinctly heard than the voices (it sounds somewhat like *obbligati* castanets, only louder); and yet in spite of this the voices are never together."

In Milan, Mendelssohn looked up Beethoven's former pupil, Dorothea von Ertmann. She and her husband, an army general, were both friendly to the young pianist. They showed him the city and entertained him with parties and music. He was impressed by Dorothea's playing of Beethoven's music and amused by her stories about the composer's use of candle snuffers as toothpicks. Through her, Mendelssohn met Mozart's son Karl, delighting him with renditions of his father's music.

After leaving Italy and the ocean, which he called "the finest object in Nature," Felix rubbernecked his way across the Swiss Alps, mainly on foot. He made over a hundred drawings and practiced the organ, working on Bach from memory. Returning to Munich, he wrote his G-minor piano concerto for an attractive young pianist named Delphine and performed it in a concert with his C-minor symphony and *Midsummer Night's Dream* overture. The king himself led the applause.

In Paris, Felix Mendelssohn learned, perhaps for the first time, that the magic spell of his younger days could be broken. He performed successfully in concerts at the Paris Conservatoire, but attempts to have the Conservatory orchestra play his *Reformation Symphony* ended in failure. In addition, two of his good friends died while he was in Paris and he succumbed to a cholera epidemic that swept the city.

After his recovery, Mendelssohn left for the "dear, old, smoky nest" of London. Once more, his music, playing, and improvisation on the organ of St. Paul's Cathedral met with acclaim. But here, too, he received sad news: Zelter, his friend and former teacher, had died in Germany.

This death led indirectly to the deepest disappointment of Mendelssohn's life. His father persuaded him to apply for Zelter's position as director of Berlin's Singakademie. Despite the fact that Felix had conducted this group in a memorable performance of Bach's *St. Matthew Passion* when only 20 years old, he was passed over for a less competent musician.

The unfortunate reason for this slight seems to have been that the majority of those voting felt that an institution presenting Christian music should not have a Jewish director. Although his ancestors were Jewish, Felix was brought up a Christian and remained true to his beliefs--as well as to his heritage--all his life. He wrote music for the Catholic and Protestant churches, and for the Jewish Synagogue. The injustice of this decision in Berlin cut too deeply to ever completely heal. Even his eventual appointment as official composer to the king could not change his attitude toward the city.

Mendelssohn began to establish himself in other parts of Germany. He conducted the Lower Rhenish Festival in Düsseldorf and in Cologne. In 1835, he became conductor of the Leipzig Gewandhaus orchestra, making a monumental contribution to the music of this city. He often conducted music by Bach, Beethoven, Mozart, and Schumann. He engaged Liszt to perform. He directed a campaign for a monument to Johann Sebastian Bach, who had served so many years in Leipzig.

Perhaps Mendelssohn's greatest accomplishment here was the founding of the Leipzig Conservatory. He engaged well-known musicians as teachers. He himself taught piano, ensemble, and composition although he felt inadequate as an instructor since he lacked patience and possessed a temper. He is reported to have yelled at one unfortunate student, "You crazy fellow--the cats play like that." Many, however, considered him an excellent teacher.

An important personal event of the Leipzig years was his marriage to a beautiful girl named Cecile, whom he met when he directed a chorus in Frankfurt. Not particularly musical, she nevertheless became a helpful wife to Felix and a good mother to their five children.

In England, there were numerous highlights, such as dining with Charles Dickens and tea at Buckingham Palace. A letter describes the palace visit and mentions that as Queen Victoria entered the room where Mendelssohn and Prince Albert waited, a draft from the open door sent music flying all over the floor. So the three of them scrambled about picking up stray sheets of music.

After this "icebreaker," Mendelssohn played "*How Lovely are the Messengers.*" The royal couple sang along with him and the prince changed the organ stops as the music demanded. When they moved to another room to look for some of the composer's songs, they had to evict a parrot before the queen could sing. "Otherwise he screams louder than I do," Her Royal Highness explained. She then sang "with utterly charming purity, strictly in time," a song written by Fanny and one by Felix. After this, the prince sang and Mendelssohn improvised. As he left the palace, he received a gold ring inscribed "Victoria Regina 1842."

Excited by this royal happening, the musician dismissed his cab and walked home in the rain. The following day, he played his D-minor piano concerto and conducted the *Hebrides* overture. The audience demanded that each be repeated.

In 1847, upon arriving home from a trip to England, Mendelssohn learned that his sister Fanny had died. They had been close all their lives and her sudden death broke his heart. Even a trip to the Switzerland he loved could not restore his health.

Felix Mendelssohn worked hard all thirty-eight years of his life. As a child, he arose every morning at 5 a.m. In addition to performing, conducting, and teaching, he revised many of his compositions several times. They range from the highly personal musical poetry called *Songs Without Words* to the religious oratorio *Elijah*. They include symphonies, concertos, overtures, chamber and church music, theatre music, organ compositions, and piano music.

One of the so-called Romantic composers, Mendelssohn lived during a time of change. By 1830, the piano had become a brilliant and expressive instrument. Hammers and strings were heavier and metal frames were in use. With perfection of the damper pedal, notes could be blended much as a painter mixes his colors. Playing the piano could be a more personal matter than playing the harpsichord, for it could be done with greater expression. And just as the feelings of the performer had become more important, so had those of the composer. Music flowed as glibly from the heart as from the head, though with Mendelssohn, form always retained its importance.

The music and playing of Felix Mendelssohn were almost always greeted with enthusiasm. A friend who was also a pianist wrote, "He played the piano as a lark soars, because it was his nature. . . . When he sat at the piano music poured out of him with the richness of inborn genius--he was a centaur and the piano his steed."

In speaking of his delicate touch, an English musician said that "his fingers seemed to be like feathers." He added that Mendelssohn electrified his audiences, casting a spell over them.

9. FRÉDÉRIC CHOPIN

In 1820, about a year after the birth of Felix Mendelssohn, Frédéric Chopin was born in Zelazowa-Wola, a village near Warsaw, Poland. His French father, Nicholas, and Polish mother, Justina, met when they worked for the Countess Skarbeck. Nicholas served as a tutor, and Justina, of noble birth herself, as a lady-in-waiting to the countess.

Soon after their marriage, the Chopins moved to Warsaw, where the father taught French and literature. He played the flute and violin; she played the piano and sang. Their first child was a girl named "Ludwika," the second a boy they nicknamed "Frycek." Because the baby boy cried when he heard music, the family thought he disliked it. Soon, he begged his sister to teach him to play. Later his mother took over the lessons.

At the age of six, Frycek began to study with a professional teacher. Zywny carried a large, square pencil that he used sometimes for disciplinary purposes, sometimes for writing down the child's compositions. He introduced his pupil to *The Well-Tempered Clavier* of J.S. Bach.

Five days after his eighth birthday, Frycek appeared in a public concert. Wearing a dark velvet jacket with a broad white collar, short trousers, and white stockings, he played a piano concerto by Gyrowetz. His mother could not attend the concert, but upon his return, she asked what the audience had liked best. "My collar, mamma, my collar," he told her.

Life at the Chopin home never became dull. Sometimes six or eight boarders, including the piano teacher, lived there. Many distinguished musicians, poets, actors, and scientists were guests. They made music, played whist (a card game), or took part in lively discussions.

At the age of twelve, Frédéric began to study composition with Joseph Elsner, the director of the newly opened Warsaw Conservatory. He had already published his first Polonaise, dedicated to the Countess Victoire Skarbeck. Other short pieces included a *Military March* that had been arranged and played by the City Governor's Band.

The following year, Madame Skarbeck invited the Chopins to spend the summer at Zelazowa-Wola. Here, in the evening, everyone gathered around the piano that had been rolled out under the chestnut trees. On the nights when they staged a show of some kind, Frédéric, a great mimic, often appeared disguised as a well-known character. At meetings of the *Literary Entertainment Society*, President Frédéric presided, and each member recited his own works. Sisters Ludwika and Emilia both wrote poetry.

When Frédéric was fifteen, he played for the Russian king of Poland, Tsar Alexander, receiving a diamond ring he would treasure all his life. Soon after this momentous occasion, the talented boy entered the Conservatory and settled down to the serious business of becoming a musician. His efforts were spurred on by such events as concerts by Hummel and by the virtuoso violinist, Paganini. In Berlin with a friend, he attended several lavish opera productions. At a reception there, he saw Felix Mendelssohn. "I couldn't summon the courage to speak to him," he confessed in a letter.

With four of his classmates, he traveled to Vienna, where he met Haslinger (Beethoven's adjutant), Gyrowetz, and Czerny. Playing mostly his own music, Chopin gave two concerts. He used a Graff piano, although Stein had offered one of his. Both concerts met with success and received encouraging reviews. But he heard for the first time the criticism that would haunt his short career: he played too softly for a large concert hall.

At the age of nineteen, Chopin composed his first etudes and the Piano Concerto in F minor, performing the concerto in two Warsaw concerts. After the first concert, the "soft playing" ghost emerged again. One reviewer advised him to show more energy. "So," he writes, "I considered very carefully where this energy should come from, and at my second concert I played, not on my own piano, but on a Viennese instrument." The critics seemed satisfied.

While composing his next piano concerto, he worried lest it prove too original and too difficult for the composer himself. But Frédéric played it in a third Warsaw concert only six months after the second. "I was not the least bit nervous," he reported. He used a Streicher piano, and the newspapers came out with excellent reviews.

Shortly after this concert, Chopin set out once more for Vienna. Friends accompanied him as far as Zelazowa-Wola, where a surprise party awaited him. A group of male Conservatory students sang a cantata with guitar accompaniment, written by his composition teacher. A banquet-- complete with speeches--followed the music.

Chopin then left Poland, never to return. But he took with him a part of his native land that was to color all his music. He saw his parents only once more, when they met for a holiday in Carlsbad. Yet he never forgot them, nor did he ever forget his Polish nationality.

From the beautiful city of Dresden, Frédéric wrote the family of a visit to the famous Picture Gallery. Certain paintings made him feel as though he were listening to music. He had been amused by a trip to a concert in a "funny sort of a box"--a sedan chair. "I laughed at myself on the way, being carried by those bearers in livery; I was greatly tempted to stamp out the bottom, but restrained myself."

In Vienna, Chopin visited Czerny, finding him hard at work on something for eight pianos. He went to the theatre and to Graff's piano shop, where he limbered up his fingers every day.

Titus, the friend who accompanied Frédéric to Vienna, returned home when he heard the news that the Polish people had revolted against Russian domination in Warsaw. Chopin felt he, too, should go. Titus finally convinced him he could do more good for his country with music than by fighting.

Partly because of the political situation and partly because of being young and alone, he grew restless. As Mozart at the same age had lingered in Mannheim, Chopin tarried in Vienna. He attended operas and concerts. He gave two concerts himself, after letting the whiskers grow on the right cheek, the one on the audience side. Hummel's son painted his portrait,

"...seated in my dressing gown on a piano stool with an inspired look on my face--where that comes from I don't know." He tried out a new parlor trick: mimicking the Viennese generals.

Finally, in July of 1831, he set out for Paris.

Zelazowa-Wola, Chopin's birthplace

10. CHOPIN: The Paris Years

Chopin quickly fell in love with the city of Paris. In addition to the opera, theatre, and concert halls, it had numerous salons where the 'intellectual greats' displayed their sundry talents. Many prominent people in the arts and sciences lived here, including a colony of wealthy Polish aristocrats. Paris seemed custom-made for Frédéric Chopin.

At 27 boulevard Poissonière, the gifted musician found a delightful fifth-floor apartment with "elegant mahogany furniture." His balcony presented a view that extended "from Montmartre to the Pantheon and all along the finest districts."

Chopin gave his first public concert in Paris after being there only six months. It took place in a hall that can still be seen today, that of the French piano manufacturer, Pleyel. Two female singers, an oboist, and five other pianists took part, including Mendelssohn. Chopin played his Concerto in F minor and Variations in B-flat. The six pianists performed a work by Kalkbrenner, one of the leading composers in Paris. Chopin used a "monochord piano, which is tiny, but its tone carries, like little bells on a giraffe." Liszt sat in the audience, ears akimbo. He was impressed, finding the poetic feeling and artistry truly special.

Chopin launched his teaching career--he called it his "mill"--after meeting Baron Rothschild. The baroness became a pupil, setting an example for titled ladies bent on keeping up with the Rothschilds. The first lessons of the day often started at 8 a.m. The teacher always dressed well, had his hair curled and his shoes polished. He used two pianos: a Pleyel grand and a small instrument at which he himself presided. When he did not feel well--which was all too often--he would lie on his couch and rub his head with *eau de cologne*. The lesson lasted at least an hour, and the fee was to be left on the mantle. The ladies frequently brought him violets. He had only one talented pupil, Karl Filtsch, who died at the age of fifteen.

His social circle consisted not only of the nobility, but of many gifted people, also. It included poets, artists, musicians, writers and scientists. He was friendly with Liszt, Mendelssohn, Schumann, Berlioz, and many dimmer lights in the music world. Once, in Liszt's apartment, Chopin answered the door wearing a blonde wig and a suit of Liszt's. His imitation proved so perfect that the visitor mistook him for Liszt and made an appointment.

Of Liszt's playing, Chopin stated that he would like to steal from Liszt the way he played his own etudes. He and Liszt sometimes played duets together. With Hiller they performed Bach's concerto for three keyboards at a Conservatoire concert. When Chopin met Moscheles, they became friends. Playing together for the court of Louis-Philippe they were a hit with both the king and the queen.

In Leipzig, Chopin visited Mendelssohn and Schumann. On this occasion, Mendelssohn played his *St. Paul*, and Chopin his newest etudes and latest concerto. Clara Schumann presented her husband's new Sonata in F minor and two of Chopin's etudes. The composer told her she was the only woman in Germany who knew how to play his music.

Chopin spent several summers at the country place of George Sand, a novelist who distinguished herself by wearing trousers and smoking cigars. Talented people were attracted to her, and many of them gathered at Nohant. Here they played charades and put on pantomimes and plays. Delacroix, an artist and friend of Frédéric, was a guest one summer. He described the place as "delightful. . . . When we are not together for dinner, lunch, billiards or walks, one can read in one's room or sprawl on one's sofa. Every now and then there blows in through your window, opening on to the garden, a breath of the music of Chopin who is at work in his room, and it mingles with the song of the nightingales and the scent of the roses."

At Nohant, Chopin wrote or perfected many of his compositions. Just as Mendelssohn did, Chopin revised constantly. He said he always thought his ideas were perfect until he wrote them down.

His preludes have been called "the most poetic work of the greatest poet among composers." They were completed and polished in a romantic setting in Majorca. For nearly two months, he lived in a deserted monastery on a high cliff that overlooked the Mediterranean. The cell was sparsely furnished: a cot, an "old square grubby box" to write on, and a candle in a lead candlestick. Over his bed glittered a Moorish filigree rose window. Outside, orange trees, cypresses and palms stretched toward the sky.

The beauty of this exotic place was equalled only by the sad effect of the climate upon his already poor health. Most of his life he battled tuberculosis and, as Beethoven had, he proved that success could be achieved despite the suffering.

A pupil recorded in her diary that one morning, after Chopin had played from memory fourteen of Bach's preludes and fugues, she expressed admiration. "That," he told her, "one never forgets," adding that for a year he had not had the energy to practice a full quarter of an hour.

Chopin rarely performed in public. Crowds frightened him, and in his lifetime he gave only about thirty public concerts. His intimate, delicate playing came off best in a salon.

In April of 184,1 George Sand wrote a well-known singer: "A great astounding piece of news is that little Chip-Chip is going to give a Grrrrand Concert. His friends have plagued him so much that he has given way. However, he imagined that it would be so difficult to arrange that he would have to give it up. But things moved more quickly than he bargained for ... and there is no more amusing sight than our meticulous and irresolute Chip-Chip compelled to keep his promise. . . . Mr. Ernst will scrape his splendid violin, and so there you are. This Chopinesque nightmare will take place at Pleyel's rooms on the 26th. He will have nothing to do with posters or prógrammes and does not want a large audience. He wants to have the affair kept quiet. So many things alarm him that I suggest that he should play without candles or audience and on a dumb keyboard. . . ."

At his final concert at Pleyel's hall on February 16, 1848, flowers decorated the staircase. The room seated 300, and nearly everyone present was a personal friend. Chopin started practicing five days in advance on the instrument he would be using. This concert marked not only the end of his career in France, but the end of an era. The following week, Louis-Philippe was dethroned. The French revolution ended all recitals for quite some time.

In April, Chopin left for London, where he received royal treatment from his pupil, Jane Stirling, and from her sister. Three pianos graced his room: a Broadwood, a Pleyel, and an Erard. But the pianist complained that he had no time to play them because of his many visitors. He played for Queen Victoria and Prince Albert and gave several public concerts in England and Scotland.

The climate did not agree with him, and in November, Chopin returned to Paris in a state of exhaustion. He had written ahead to ask that a bouquet of violets be placed in his drawing-room. This he felt would add a "little poetry" to his Paris home.

Chopin died not quite a year later. Some three thousand invited guests attended his funeral. The Funeral March from his B-flat minor Piano Sonata was played as bearers carried his coffin up the aisle of the Madeleine. An organist played transcriptions of his E-minor and B-minor preludes. The orchestra and chorus of the Conservatoire performed the Mozart Requiem.

Frédéric Chopin's gift to the world consists of piano music that has been revered for over a hundred years. It includes a fantasie, ballades, scherzos, mazurkas, waltzes, polonaises, etudes, preludes, impromptus, sonatas, rondos, 2 piano concertos, and nocturnes (once called "sighs" by the English).

Chopin intended to write a book on teaching and had made notes on the subject. He considered fingering and good hand position extremely important. Of the pedal, he admonished a friend to be careful "because this is a sensitive and awfully noisy rascal. You must treat it politely and delicately." He suggested that the preludes and fugues of J.S. Bach be played every day. "If you have plenty of time memorize Bach; only by memorizing a work does one become able to play it perfectly."

One of Chopin's pupil's wrote, "His playing was always noble and beautiful, his tones always sang, whether in full *forte* or in the softest *piano*."

Frédéric Chopin, as painted by his friend Delacroix

The young Liszt,
from a pencil drawing by Ingres

11. FRANZ LISZT

Franz Liszt won his first admiring glances--from his mother and father --on October 22, 1811. He spent his early childhood in Hungary, where his father worked as a farm superintendent for the Esterhazy properties in Raiding. The elder Liszt had played cello in Franz Joseph Haydn's orchestra at the summer palace of the Esterhazys. He also played piano, violin, and sang bass. Chamber music graced many an evening in the one-story brick house with its tall chimneys.

Because Franz was not a healthy child, he did not receive his first piano lesson until he was six years old. After three months, his father had to discontinue the instruction because of the boy's recurring fever. At the age of eight, he was taken to Vienna to play for Carl Czerny, who wrote of the occasion: "He was a pale, delicate-looking child and while playing swayed in the chair as if drunk, so that I often thought he would fall to the floor. Moreover his playing was completely irregular, careless and confused, and he had so little knowledge of correct fingering that he threw his fingers all over the keyboard in an altogether arbitrary fashion. Nevertheless, I was amazed by the talent with which Nature herself had equipped him. I gave him a few things to sightread, which he did, purely by instinct, but for that very reason in a manner that revealed that Nature herself had here created a pianist. . . . Never before had I so eager, talented or industrious a student."

Czerny agreed to take the child as pupil, and from then on his mother and father struggled to find the means. Prince Nicholas II, for whom Adam worked, offered to pay for the lessons but refused to transfer Adam to a position in Vienna. Finally, Franz gave a concert in the home of Count Michael Esterhazy. The nine-year-old prodigy dazzled the local nobility, and a group of them agreed to make annual contributions for six years. Because of faith in their son's ability, the parents decided to move to Vienna. Adam gave up his position, and Anna apparently gave up her savings. In later years, Liszt is said to have marveled at their courage.

At first, the child must have wondered about the wisdom of a move to Vienna. Czerny prescribed a stiff and exclusive dose of scales and technical exercises. He concentrated on fingering, rhythm, and tone quality. When the patient finally rebelled, "Dr." Czerny added a supplemental dose of Clementi sonatas and, eventually, a taste of Bach, Hummel, Beethoven, and Moscheles. After the Liszts moved to the Krugerstrasse--Czerny's street--young Franz had a lesson each evening without charge. He also received free theory and composition instruction from the much maligned Salieri--once falsely accused of poisoning Mozart.

After fourteen months with Czerny and two public concerts in Vienna, Franz and his parents started out on a concert tour. The twelve-year-old took with him a small silent keyboard on which to practice while riding in the carriage. They went to Munich, Stuttgart, Strasbourg, and Paris, where "Le petit Liszt" dazzled his audiences. They thought his playing equalled that of Johann Hummel and Ignaz Moscheles.

In Paris and in England, he played on "the new Grand Piano Forte, invented by Sebastian Erard." It had a compass of seven octaves and a new action that allowed a performer to repeat notes at a greater speed than was previously possible. Franz played a Hummel concerto, and at the end he improvised on a theme suggested by a lady "in the stalls." The concert created such excitement that George V issued a royal invitation to play at the palace. After a tour to the French provinces, Liszt returned to London.

Franz was sixteen when his father died. From then on he supported himself. He and his mother moved to an apartment in Paris. Almost immediately, pupils flocked to his studio. Some days he taught from nine in the morning to nine at night.

Early in 1832, Liszt heard Paganini for the first time. Inspired by this flamboyant virtuoso, he decided to accomplish on the piano what Paganini achieved on the violin. For two years, he gave no concerts. Instead, he concentrated on practicing--to the tune of at least ten hours a day, with four of five of them spent on exercises.

He amazed all the great pianists, even Moscheles and Mendelssohn. A contemporary wrote that Liszt was "all sunshine and dazzling splendor. . . . For him there were no difficulties of execution, the most incredible seeming child's play under his fingers. One of the transcendent merits of his playing was the crytal-like clearness which never failed him for a moment, even in the most complicated and, for anyone else, impossible passage. . . . The power he drew from his instrument was such as I have never heard since, but never harsh. . . ."

Many stories have been told about the artist's incredible ability as a sightreader. He could read through the most difficult numbers without error, even when they were in barely legible manuscript. Some considered his first reading the best, since the second time he could become bored and make additions of his own. One writer relates that "he indulged in fiddle-faddle of this kind even in such a work as the *Kreutzer Sonata* of Beethoven."

Liszt is credited with giving the first complete programs without help from other performers, calling these recitals "Soliloquies." He receives the bouquet (floral or otherwise, depending upon your point of view) for introducing the practice of performing from memory. He was also first to consistently place the piano with the sound directed toward the auditorium. Audiences were asked to deposit themes for improvisation in a chalice in the lobby.

When still in his twenties Liszt met his leading rival, "Old Arpeggio" Thalberg. This pianist derived his nickname from his trick of bringing out the melody in the middle register with both thumbs, embroidering it with arpeggios above and below. Some thought he must have three hands.

Except for visits to Nohant and a few romantic summers on a small island in the Rhine, Liszt spent most of his time dashing around Europe giving concerts. When the Danube overflowed its banks and brought suffering to Hungary, he left Italy for Vienna. He gave several recitals, donating the proceeds to the flood victims. Later, in the same manner, he raised money for a statue of Beethoven erected in Bonn.

Franz Liszt's arrival in Berlin threw the city into a dither. His portrait looked out from numerous shop windows. He gave 21 concerts in two months. Liszt, tall and handsome, would march regally onto the stage, shaking his long locks and rattling the many medals on his lapel. Women rushed forward and fought over the green doeskin gloves he removed and placed on the piano. They tossed their jewels to him and yelled and screamed. Or they fainted! They collected souvenirs: broken strings, snuff boxes, dregs from his coffee that they carried in phials. One admirer fished a cigar butt out of an ash tray and carried it on her bosom until the day she died.

Liszt relished the role of a glittering star and played his part with flair. From Berlin he made a grand exit in a coach drawn by six white horses, followed by 30 carriages with four horses each. The first concert here was attended by 3,000.

In Kiev he met the second great love of his life, a princess. His first love was a countess, and one of their daughters married Richard Wagner. Liszt also involved himself in many minor romances and flirtations.

At the height of his popularity he gave up playing for profit and became musical director for the Weimar Court, where he lived in a palace. He conducted music written by Schumann, Chopin, Weber, Berlioz, and Wagner as well as that of Haydn, Mozart, and Beethoven, making the already famous literary center of Weimar a musical center as well. According to one reviewer he "disclosed a deep understanding of all the works he conducted," allowing "the inner spirit of the music to shine in all its splendor." Someone else called him Germany's most talented and energetic conductor. He directed both operas and concerts.

The famous Weimar piano classes were held from 4 to 6 p.m. on Tuesdays, Thursdays, and Saturdays, and were open to everyone without charge. Teachers arrived from all over the world, sometimes for only a class of two. Then they might return home and advertise themselves as pupils of Liszt.

Weimar housed so many musicians when Liszt was in residence that the city passed an ordinance against practicing with open windows. Offenders paid a fine of three marks, but since it could be collected only once a day, many paid it early in the morning and practiced in peace the rest of the day.

The Master took keen interest in his students, often finding positions for them. If he learned a pupil was leaving for financial reasons, a purse of money found its way to the student's room. Equally generous with his time, Liszt looked at many manuscripts and wrote many letters. At the age of 70, he confided, "My dislike of letters has become immense. How can I answer more than 2,000 a year without losing my reason?"

On concert tours, the virtuoso pianist had done almost no composing except for transcriptions such as those of the Beethoven symphonies. In Weimar, he found time for original compositions: piano pieces, symphonic poems, concertos, and other choral and orchestral music. The grandiose manner so characteristic of his playing--and his daily living--permeated much of his music. What Schumann referred to as the "tinsel," upset many of Liszt's friends who were musicians. Except for Wagner, most of them deserted him.

As a teenager, Liszt had often thought about the religious life. Both his mother and father had argued that his talent belonged to art, not the Church. When he reached the age of fifty, he gave up his post in the "city of Muses" and began to spend much of his time in Rome. Eventually he received four of the seven degrees of priesthood and was called Abbé Liszt, although he could not hear confessions or celebrate mass.

In 1875, Liszt became director of the Budapest Musical Academy, founded in his honor by the Hungarian government. From then on he divided his time between Rome, Weimar, and Budapest.

In celebration of his seventy-fifth year, Liszt went to Paris and London. Even at this age he could still hypnotize his audiences and charm them with his magic. He played for Queen Victoria at Windsor Castle and attended a reception in his honor at the Grosvenor Gallery.

After returning from England, Liszt went to Bayreuth for the Wagnerian festivities. On the train he caught a cold that turned to pneumonia. He died in Bayreuth and was buried there.

An anecdote related by Amy Fay in her entertaining book titled *Music Study in Germany* highlights one facet of Liszt's complex personality. The author writes of a public appearance in which "He was rolling up the piano in arpeggios in a very grand manner indeed, when he struck a semi-tone short of the high note which he had intended to end. . . . A half smile came across his face, as much as to say--'Don't fancy that *this* little thing disturbs me'--and he instantly went meandering down the piano in harmony with the false note he had struck, and then rolled deliberately up in a second grand sweep, this time striking true."

Franz Liszt was not only a great pianist--he was a magnetic showman who won admiring glances all his life.

12. CLARA WIECK

While visiting Vienna in 1838, Liszt received an invitation to a musical soirée at Thalberg's home. Here he met a nineteen-year-old girl whose piano playing impressed him. The admiration was mutual, for Clara Wieck wrote a friend, "Since hearing and seeing Liszt's pyrotechnics I feel like a school girl. My own playing bores me. I think I ought to stop touring altogether. . . ."

The first entry in Volume I of Clara's 45 journals appears in her father's handwriting. It reads: "I was born in Leipzig, September 13, 1819--and received the name of Clara Josephine." As soon as she could write, the child was forced to make her own record of events and reactions, a practice continued throughout her life.

Both of Clara's parents were musicians. Her mother sang and played in public and taught piano. Her father, also a teacher, maintained a music-lending library and a piano agency. The fact that most of Clara's early years were spent with a nursemaid described as "kindly but dumb" may account for the child's not beginning to talk at the normal age.

After her mother and father were divorced, Clara remained with her father. At the age of five, she had her first piano lesson and was assigned to a class with two other girls known to be chatterboxes. Almost immediately, her vocal chords swung into action, although she knew notes and rhythm before she could count or recite the alphabet. She had a daily lesson after school and was then required to practice two hours, dividing the time into several brief periods. Her father believed long sessions led to wandering minds and fingers. She could not, however, waste time reading.

For her eighth birthday Clara was allowed to select a new grand piano. She chose a Stein. The young pianist had "earned" this gift by playing Mozart's Concerto in E-flat Major with a chamber orchestra of two violins, two violas, two horns, a cello, and a flute. For the occasion she wore a new dress with large puffed sleeves, small gold tassel earrings, and, in her dark hair, a ribbon. A letter to her mother reported, "Everything went quite well and I didn't get stuck. Only my cadenza wouldn't come off right away, where I had to repeat a chromatic scale three times, yet it didn't scare me at all." The child added that she hoped to visit her mother soon and play four-hand music with her.

Following this triumph, Clara's teacher permitted a few days' relief from daily lessons. But nine days later, she still seemed to be resting on her laurels. The journal entry read: "My father, who had hoped in vain for a change in my disposition, noticed again today that I am still lazy, listless, disorderly, headstrong, and disobedient, and that I play as badly as I study. I played Hünten's variations Opus 2 to him so badly, without even repeating the first part of the variation, that he tore up the copy before my eyes, and from today onwards he will not give me another hour."

For a week, Clara practiced only scales and exercises. Finally reinstated because she had faithfully promised to improve, she was soon practicing three hours a day, still in short sessions. She had developed perfect pitch and knew enough about harmony to improvise.

When nine years old, Clara made her debut at the Gewandhaus. She played the treble part of a duet with one of her father's pupils. Despite an incident that might have unnerved a seasoned performer, she "won much applause." She had been picked up by the wrong carriage and found herself on the way to a country ball. When she finally arrived at the concert hall tearfully topsy-turvy, her teacher fed her sugarplums and the comforting assurance, "I quite forgot to tell you, Clärchen, that people are always taken to the wrong house the first time they play in public."

At the age of eleven, Clara Wieck soloed with the Gewandhaus orchestra amd played a composition of her own. Her journal reads: "I played to the satisfaction of my father, and of the public. My bows were not very successful, except fot the first; they were too quick." Critics praised her performance, and she was payed thirty thalers, ten of which were hers to keep. In the diary, she promised "to treat my family frequently at the Kuchengarten."

The young pianist played in private homes and for Pagannini, who made yearly visits to Leipzig. Soon, Herr Wieck began to think about taking his prodigy to Paris. Plans had to be postponed when Clara broke out with the measles. But this gave her extra time to work on her French. Papa Wieck's daughter never wasted time. On their way to Paris, they stopped in Weimar, where Clara's playing impressed the great Goethe. "This fragile maid has the strength of six boys," observed the poet.

In Paris, the Wiecks encountered the usual resistance to outsiders, but they sat in the audience at Pleyel's when Chopin gave his first Paris concert. He played his Variations, Opus 2, which Clara had already mastered and presented on various occasions. She performed at a soirée given by a princess, and Paganini agreed to appear in a public concert with her. But the violinist became ill, cholera broke out in Paris, and many left the city to escape the disease. Clara played her concert without music in accordance with Paris custom, and wrestled with the heavy action of the Paris pianos as well as with many keys that stuck. Despite the delicate touch taught by her father--who insisted everything be played musically--Clara accepted the challenge and did herself proud. Back in Leipzig after seven months, she gave two concerts in the Gewandhaus, introducing the Paris custom of playing without music.

On her thirteenth birthday, Clara got stuck in the middle of a scherzo she was playing as a forfeit. Her excuse: "No wonder! With nobody but a lot of little girls for an audience, and to have to play piano on my birthday."

The day she became seventeen, Clara encountered a more serious problem. On her way to a concert in Naumberg, her carriage overturned. She received cuts and bruises, and her dress was torn. Being a real trouper, she gave her concert and sang two songs. Later the same year, she gave six successful concerts in Vienna where she received great acclaim.

Clara Wieck used only a few assisting artists in her concerts, instead of following the custom of hiring an orchestra and soloists. Her taste in music was improved by contact with one of her father's pupils, Herr Robert Schumann. He urged her to include only the best music on her programs. Except for the composer himself, Clara was probably the first famous pianist to play Chopin's music in public.

Clara's interest in Schumann blossomed gradually, starting as a tiny bud and opening petal by petal. As a child, she enjoyed his tales of ghosts and robbers as well as his music. When she grew older, they fell deeply in love. But their plans for marriage--or even meeting--were frequently upended by her father. They endured long separations, sometimes exchanging notes using a maid as a go-between.

Wieck, who considered Robert's future too insecure for his talented daughter, feared marriage would end her promising career. Clara loved her father and realized she owed her success to his careful training. Because of this, the long battle to win his approval of their marriage proved particularly painful to her--and to the sensitive composer. Some of Wieck's charges were true but absurd, condemning Schumann because "he speaks so softly," or "no one can read his writing." Other accusations, more serious, were simply untrue. Herr Wieck floundered about like a freshly caught fish, splashing malicious slander in every direction. Finally, Robert and Clara were forced to seek permission from the court for their marriage. The case dragged on for over a year.

Through all the agony and anxiety, Clara relied upon a strong constitution and "great faith in God." She put up with the hardships of touring, sometimes worrying about programs, pianos, or the unstable state of Robert's health. In Berlin, she herself collapsed under the strain, writing Robert, "I only began to work seriously at your sonata (for the first time) yesterday, and I have to play it tomorrow. . . . "

A letter from Hamburg revealed, " . . . for the whole day I had to run about looking for a piano, as there are very few here, and no good ones." She played first on "an old one . . . now quite played out," then on one "so stiff; if only I can get through my pieces!" Finally she happened upon a "wonderful instrument of Andreas Stein's of Vienna . . . at my service for the whole of my stay in Hamburg."

Clara found time to compose, publishing a piano concerto and, in Paris, writing "Three Romances for the Piano dedicated to Monsieur Robert Schumann." But the concert pianist missed news of her family. It hurt her that her stepmother "should never even think of writing me. I never hear anything of the dear little girls; it is as if I had no family left."

After her own mother stepped into the breach, Clara enjoyed the companionship and encouragement denied her as a child. Additional cheer radiated from an occasional meeting with Robert and from his letters. He wrote her often and frequently included new piano music or songs.

The July 4, 1840, entry to her diary reveals another delightful surprise: "This evening as I came home, what did I find? A beautiful Härtel grand piano, wreathed with flowers, and in the next room, there sat he, the dear, most warmly loved Robert. . . . A dainty poem lay among the flowers."

The day before her twenty-first birthday, Clara Wieck and Robert Schumann were married at Schönefeld, near Leipzig. The bride recorded in her diary: "It was a day without a jar, and I may thus enter it in this book as the fairest and most momentous of my life."

Clara Wieck at age 13
E. Fechner

Robert Schumann
(1810-1856)

13. DR. and MRS. SCHUMANN

By the time he and Clara were married, Robert Schumann had given birth to a number of musical brain children. They included *Carnaval*, *Scenes from Childhood*, *Davidsbündlertänze*, and a shower of songs written the year of his marriage. He had also requested and received an honorary doctor's degree, which he hoped would impress his bride-to-be and her father.

Having given up the study of law, Robert set out to become a concert pianist, but the sling he wore in the hope of playing faster sooner only lamed his hand. He became, as he said, "nine-fingered me." So he turned to composition.

Robert also edited a magazine that encouraged promising new composers. Unlike Beethoven, who once remarked that if he wanted to listen to contemporary music, he would listen to his own, Schumann appreciated much of the music of his time. Favorite composers included Schubert, Chopin, and Mendelssohn. He discovered the manuscript of Schubert's C-Major Symphony and arranged to have it published. After hearing it rehearsed, he wrote Clara, "I have been in Paradise today." A Chopin composition he greeted with, "Hats off, gentlemen! A genius!" Mendelssohn he proclaimed "the one to whom I look as a lofty mountain."

Felix and Robert met when Mendelssohn became director at the Gewandhaus. Both in their twenties, they shared a love for the music of J.S. Bach and the writings of Jean Paul Richter. Before their marriages, they saw each other almost daily, often having lunch together. They kept in touch all their lives, and Schumann served as one of the pallbearers at Mendelssohn's funeral.

When the newlyweds settled down in Leipzig, they started keeping a diary together. One of Clara's entries concerned her fear of practicing, even though they had two grand pianos in separate rooms. Because of "the evils of thin walls," the pianist felt she might disturb the composer. When Robert read this, he tried to make certain that she practiced more. But, with household duties and an ever-increasing family, Clara frequently worried about "getting behind" in her practicing. As she said, "If I rest, I rust."

The two found time for studying musical form together. They analyzed the *Well-Tempered Clavier*, Beethoven overtures, symphonies, chamber music, and piano sonatas. On alternate weeks, they studied Shakespeare.

Both musicians kept their counterpoint sharpened by writing fugues. On Christmas Eve, Clara presented her new husband with three songs she had written. That same December, Robert started working on a symphony, using a rusty steel pen he had found at Beethoven's grave in Vienna. The following March, Mendelssohn conducted this *Spring Symphony* at a Gewandhaus concert. Clara made her debut as Frau Schumann at the same concert, playing works of Schumann, Chopin, Mendelssohn, Scarlatti, and Thalberg. Robert was delighted with his first attempt at orchestration--he had help from Felix--and decided to "follow this road further." "My next symphony shall be called 'Clara,' and in it I will paint her picture with flutes, oboes, and harps," he promised.

True to his word, Robert surprised his wife on her twenty-second birthday with another symphony. She had just presented him with their first child, a daughter they called Marie. The second symphony, which after revision became the fourth, was performed at the Gewandhaus in December. Clara and Liszt played duets on the same program.

Concerts of Schumann's music and Clara's playing became popular, and invitations were received from other parts of Germany, and Holland. Robert soon tired of the traveling, as it left little time for composing. Finally he left for home, and Clara went to Copenhagen without him. She had her first sea voyage, and she wrote, "It felt horrible as we left land." About Hans Christian Anderson, whom she met and liked, a letter stated, "He has a poetic and childlike disposition. He is fairly young, but very ugly."

In February of 1844 the couple started out on tour again. They stopped first in Berlin, where they were guests of the Mendelssohns. Frau Mendelssohn gave Frau Schumann a pair of fur cuffs to protect her wrists from the chill of the Russian climate. Clara wore them on stage, where drafts frequently made her wrists cold and stiff. In Moscow she gave four sold-out concerts. Both musicians were well received wherever they appeared, but Robert became ill and could hardly wait to get home to tend to his note-knitting.

Upon their return, Schumann resumed his classes at the Leipzig Conservatory, where he taught piano, composition, and score-reading. He worked so hard that what he called a "weakness of the nerves" set in and left him unable to work. Neither mountain air nor the Carlsbad "cure" seemed to help. A visit to Dresden proved more beneficial, and the Schumanns decided to move there permanently.

Several farewell concerts took place in Leipzig. At one of these, Clara and Felix played selections from Mendelssohn's *Midsummer Night's Dream* music. Clara wrote: "He took the scherzo at such a pace that I didn't know where I was!"

In Dresden, Robert's health gradually improved. He began to compose fugues, then a symphony, and finally the A-minor Piano Concerto. Clara played this concerto first in Dresden and then, on New Year's Day, at the Gewandhaus.

During his frequent walks, Robert often ran into the Kapellmeister of the Court, Richard Wagner. They had little in common except a talent for music, but they would walk along together accompanied by Wagner's dog "Peps." Schumann commented upon Richard's "immense gift of the gab" that "one cannot listen to for very long," and Wagner complained about Robert's "long silences."

Communication became increasingly difficult for the composer, but because he had a large family to support, he sometimes assumed positions for which he was not constitutionally qualified. Clara, more aware of his great talent than of his limitations, encouraged him to conduct choruses in Dresden.

When Robert accepted a post as conductor of the Düsseldorf chorus and orchestra, the Schumanns moved once more. A royal welcome included flowers in their hotel room, serenades, concerts, and a three-course banquet. Here, speeches and toasts must have been more abundant than food, for the arrival of each course was greeted with a loud "Hurrah." The opening concert included Mendelssohn's G-minor Concerto, with Clara as soloist, and a flurry of trumpets to usher the Schumanns on and off stage.

For a while, things went well. They had a large house with ample room for their musical evenings. Clara resumed composing as well as practicing. Robert achieved success with his revised D-minor Symphony at the Rhine Music Festival.

Gradually it became apparent that Robert Schumann was not fitted for the task of giving directions to people, and he was eased out of his position. The affair was painful for both Clara and Robert, and it probably contributed to the composer's growing problem with anxiety.

In the midst of the unfortunate episodes, a blond, blue-eyed youth of twenty knocked on the Schumanns' door. He brought with him freshly composed music, which he played for them. The genius of young Johannes Brahms was recognized immediately. Clara gave him a few lessons in playing the piano, which helped considerably, and Robert wrote to his publisher in Leipzig about Brahms. He also made Brahms the subject of his final essay for the *Neue Zeitschrift*, calling him a "young eagle whom I should like to accompany in his first flight over the world."

Soon after Brahms' visit, Dr. and Mrs. Schumann left for a tour of Holland. Again, everywhere they were well-received, with many triumphs for both of them. In a letter to the children, Robert wrote, "Mamma is bringing a great deal of fame and lots of gold pieces with her; you will be surprised."

This man, who loved children and said they were "blessings," had already written an *Album for the Young*. The *Scenes from Childhood*, written for adults who remember their childhood, grew out of his wife's remark that he sometimes seemed like a child to her. For daughters Marie, Elise, and Julie, Robert wrote three *Sonatas for the Young* (Opus 118).

Early in 1854, the anxiety Robert had fought all his life finally won its last battle. The agony of hearing in his mind--day and night--musical sounds (often played by a full orchestra), led him to the Rhine River where he tried to drown himself. Two fishermen rescued him and returned him to his home, ending a frantic search that had been underway. A few days later, this musical genius was committed to an asylum near Bonn. In June, Clara gave birth to their eighth child, whom she named Felix in Mendelssohn's honor.

Almost immediately, at the age of thirty-five, she began to practice.

"I am haunted by music as never before; at night I cannot find sleep, and by day I am so absorbed by music that I lose track of everything else...." Clara had help with the children from Johannes who, along with her many other friends, rallied to her side. Brahms later fell in love with Clara, but she could not forget her first love. They remained good friends throughout their lives.

Clara built up a repertoire of Bach, Beethoven, Mozart, Scarlatti, Handel, Haydn, Chopin, Mendelssohn, Brahms, Robert Schumann, and a composition of her own. There were five concerts in Vienna, then performances in Budapest, Prague, Leipzig, and Dresden. In the spring of 1856, she went to England, giving twenty-six concerts, yet worrying constantly about the ups and downs of her husband's health.

Upon returning from England, Clara learned that Robert was failing rapidly. Two days before he died, she was at last permitted to see him. "He smiled, and put his arm around me with great effort, for he can no longer control his limbs. I shall never forget it," she wrote.

Robert Schumann was buried in Bonn. Clara's diary reads: "I had not let it be known, because I did not want a number of strangers to come. His dearest friends went in front, and I came (unnoticed) behind, and it was best thus; he would have liked it so. And so, with his departure, all my happiness is over."

The Gewandhaus, as painted by Felix Mendelssohn
Reproduction from the Collection of the Library of Congress

14. CLARA SCHUMANN: Concert Pianist

Despite her grief, Clara Schumann was not one to sit around and feel sorry for herself. Upon returning to Düsseldorf, she farmed out the children, packed Brahms off to Hamburg, and accepted an offer to give three recitals in Copenhagen. After a tour of England and a summer on the Rhine, she moved to Berlin.

Soon she was off again. In Munich, Clara strained a tendon in her left arm when she was carried away with enthusiasm while performing Robert's concerto. She had to cancel her remaining concerts and return to Berlin with her arm in a sling.

Her profession held another peril: that of aching joints caused by cold, drafty concert halls. Audiences often carried hot water bags and fur-lined foot bags, but this could hardly serve as the solution for the featured soloist.

What hurt her most of all was having to give concerts without Robert. Everywhere she went, she played his music and that of Johannes Brahms. In Paris, she found that interest in her husband's music had already been established. All the famous musicians came to call on her--except the great Rossini, who considered himself too important. Clara and her oldest daughter, Marie, went to *his* home. They were ushered into a waiting room where other callers "sat on very high chairs, about an immense circular table. Rossini was constantly dipping into his pockets, sometimes for a snuff box and sometimes for a box of lozenges. As he refreshed

himself, he would also press a lozenge into my hand. He is very amusing."
Clara loved England most of all, as had Mendelssohn. Twenty times she
crossed the English Channel to give concerts.

When Frau Schumann bought a cottage in Baden-Baden, she was
able to gather her brood together for the summer and, for the first time,
get to know them well. The white farm house that looked so small from
the front spread out in the back, and each member of the family had a
private room. "The country is heavenly," Clara wrote, "and we don't have
to take walks to enjoy it. "All we need to do is to look out the window."

Marie took charge of running the house, cooking, sewing, and
mending for everyone. She and her sister Elise had two piano lessons a
week from their mother and, in turn, taught the younger children. Only
Ferdinand, still in Berlin, and the retarded Ludwig, apprenticed to a
bookseller, were not there.

Life in the "Kennel," as they called their cottage, followed a pattern.
After breakfast, Clara spent an hour out in the arbor, writing letters or
perhaps chatting with a neighbor. Then she came inside, opened the grand
piano, and "the house was flooded with sound," wrote daughter Eugenie.
"Waves of sound surged like a sea, legato and staccato; in octaves, sixths,
tenths, and double thirds. Then arpeggios of all kinds, octaves, shakes . . .
exquisite modulations leading from key to key." These warm-ups were
followed by Bach fugues, Chopin etudes, Robert Schumann's compositions,
or some of Brahms' newest music.

Four o'clock in the afternoon was set aside for visitors. In the late
afternoon, they all went for a walk, perhaps stopping in an outdoor cafe
for a large sugared pancake or Clara's special favorite, a lettuce salad.
As a child, she had often interrupted her practice sessions to enjoy a few
bites of cucumber.

In the evenings, music filled the house, which was open to guests on
Wednesday nights. The pianos in the house were furnished by well-known
firms. Clara's pet instrument, a Steinweg (the original Steinway), she took
everywhere on tour except to England. There, she didn't want to offend
the generous Broadwood, who offered his pianos so freely.

Clara Schumann's birthday brought the summer reunions to a close.
Marie packed and got ready to leave on tour with her mother. The others

were dispersed to destinations such as schools or teaching positions. Because of her health, Julie took off to spend the winter on the Riviera.

Soon after the grand occasion of playing for the new German emperor, Clara joined the faculty of the Berlin Music Academy. She received a good salary, lifelong pension, five months' vacation, freedom in the selection of pupils, and permission to arrange her schedule to allow for concert engagements. Summers could still be spent at the Baden-Baden retreat.

Many important guests visited the "Kennel" every year. Brahms, who at one time gave piano lessons to Eugenie, was the most frequent visitor--always treated as one of the family. Not many years passed before Fate started to take its toll on the group. Julie, who had married a count, died first, followed a short time later by her oldest son. Ferdinand developed rheumatism and became addicted to morphine. Ludwig had to be sent to an asylum, and Felix died at the age of twenty-two. After Elise married an American, only Marie and Eugenie were left with their mother. Through all the backstage tragedies, Clara bravely kept her engagements as a concert artist.

When nearly sixty years old, she left Berlin for the Conservatory at Frankfurt, where she had help in weeding out untalented pupils. Both Marie and Eugenie were eventually appointed as assistants. Christmas parties became part of the routine here, with every pupil playing a piece and then gathering around the Christmas tree for "a punch and a lottery."

As with many another performer, she worried herself to a frazzle before concerts. Of her last appearance in England she wrote, "I was again so nervous, but closed successfully with *Carnaval*. I believe I have never played it as I did today. . . ."

Of a concert at the Frankfurt Museum when she was seventy-one, she commented: "My frame of mind for eight long days prior to the concert was absolutely ghastly. First, from one hour to the next, the dread that something might happen to me on or off stage. Then there was the fear of performing badly. My thoughts, even at night, were constantly on the Concerto, backward, forward, even while people spoke to me; it was unbearable. In spite of this I played well, perhaps never better; I felt as carefree as though sitting at home, plus the inspiration of having an audience."

Clara always rose to the occasion. This one marked her final appearance
at a regular public concert. The following year, she gave up teaching at
the Conservatory but kept a few pupils, including two of her grandchildren.

As she grew older, Clara encountered more and more problems
with her health. She developed neuritis in her hands, arms, and shoulder,
sometimes not being able to touch the piano for months. Gradually she
grew deaf, and this interfered not only with her own playing but with the
enjoyment of hearing others perform. One diary entry reads: "I tried
going to the Museum today. I wanted to hear Brahms' D Major Symphony.
But, alas, it was no use. I heard nothing except one *forte*. Everything
sounded wrong, and I could not hear the soft parts at all." In Frankfurt
she went to Wanda Landowska's harpsichord recital. She heard little but
predicted that the artist would go far.

Some of Clara's comments about other performers were not quite
as charitable. Liszt, whom she had once admired, became a favorite target.
Her diary revealed: "He gallops over the keys with superb skill, but is it
music?" Or, "I could weep over his abominable playing. . . . How Liszt
banged the instrument, and what tempi he takes!"

About Anton Rubenstein, a frequent visitor at Baden-Baden, she
wrote: "From the moment he struck the piano, I was horrified at his hard
touch, and I don't like his preliminary keyboard runs; it seems to me
unartistic to run up and down the piano in galloping thirds and sixths. His
technique, incidentally, is notable." Even her good friend Johannes was
criticized: "Unfortunately Brahms plays more awfully all the time; he does
nothing but bang the piano, cuff it, and grope for the keys. . . ." Brahms
had once been an excellent pianist but, as has been known to occur with
many musicians, he hated to practice, and didn't.

Clara Schumann was nearly seventy-seven when she died. Her artistry
had been recognized by many esteemed critics. George Bernard Shaw
described her playing as "nobly beautiful and poetic."

Another critic commented on her ability to adjust to the character
and period of whatever she performed. He added, "She could be called
the greatest living pianist, were the range of her physical strength not limited
by her sex. . . . Everything is distinct, clear, sharp as a pencil sketch."

Perhaps this "priestess of the piano" evoked special magic because she had been loved by two of the world's great musicians: Robert Schumann and Johannes Brahms.

Clara Schumann, concert pianist

Brahms at the age of twenty
Drawing by Laurens

15. JOHANNES BRAHMS

Johannes Brahms heard his first lullaby in 1833 in a poor district of Hamburg called the Specksgang, or Bacon Alley. His father played the double bass, performing on street corners in a "pass-the-hat" band, later in a theatre orchestra. His mother possessed a talent for needlework and had an exceptional memory.

Young "Hannes" particularly enjoyed playing with toy soldiers, but he willingly deserted them for music. When his father discovered his son had absolute pitch, he sent him to a local pianist for lessons. Later, the boy studied with Hamburg's "best teacher," receiving a solid foundation in harmony, counterpoint, theory, and sightreading, as well as piano.

At the age of nine, Johannes started to play for dancing in the bars near his home. Hamburg was a busy seaport. When a ship came in loaded with sailors, the pianist would be dragged from bed and sent to work. Sometimes he played all night. But he never wasted time, for he kept a book of poetry on the piano and read while playing.

Johannes earned money as a piano teacher from the time he was twelve years old. Later on he wrote, ". . . such a young lad was hardly likely to have pupils entrusted to him who could give him any particular pleasure. And yet I stood it all well enough. . . . I am convinced it did me good and was necessary for my development."

At the age of fourteen, Johannes gave a concert that included works of Bach, Beethoven, and Mendelssohn, in addition to his own variations on a folk tune. In other concerts, he assisted as a soloist or accompanist.

When Brahms set out on tour with a Hungarian violinist named Eduard

Reményi, he took no music with him. He could play everything from memory, including a Beethoven violin sonata that he once had to transpose from C-minor to C-sharp minor because the piano was tuned too low.

In Hanover, he met the famous violinist Joseph Joachim and submitted some of his music to him. It was signed "Johannes Kreisler junior." For earlier efforts Brahms used the names "G. W. Marks" and "Karl Wurth." After meeting Liszt and spending a summer on the Rhine, the youth presented himself at the Schumanns' home in Düsseldorf. Because of Robert's influence, the young musician was able to surprise his parents by placing freshly printed music under their Christmas tree.

After Robert died, Clara helped Johannes find a satisfying sinecure at the Detmold Court. He gave piano lessons to a princess and her ladies-in-waiting, conducted the court choir, and served as soloist at court concerts. This left him ample time for composing and roaming about the countryside he loved so much.

In 1859, Brahms finished the Piano Concerto in D minor, performing it in Hanover, Leipzig, and Hamburg. He reported that in Leipzig and Hanover, it "enjoyed a brilliant and decided failure." The Gewandhaus audience, it seemed, responded by hissing. Reception in Hamburg was only slightly less hostile.

When Brahms organized a ladies' chorus in his native city, he drew up a set of rules that might serve as a model for volunteer choir directors. He established a system of fines for nonattendance or late arrival at rehearsals. Listeners were to be tolerated only if they did not interfere with the rehearsal. When the group went to the country for picnics, Brahms sometimes perched on a tree limb to conduct.

After giving two piano recitals in Vienna that were well received, Brahms decided to move there. He had hoped to be appointed as conductor of the Hamburg Philharmonic, but the vacancy had been filled by someone else. As was the case with Mendelssohn, Johannes never forgot that his talents had been spurned by his native city.

For a while, Brahms conducted the Vienna Singakademie. He composed and also gave concerts in Holland, Germany, Switzerland, and Hungary. Because he was once frightened by a boating accident, he refused to cross the channel to England.

As a pianist, Brahms played forcefully and energetically. Schumann said he had a talent for "drawing orchestral or organ effects out of the instrument." He showed remarkable precision in making jumps with his left hand, perhaps because of playing for so many dancing sailors in his youth. As he found less and less time to practice, his playing deteriorated--so he didn't always try to play up to tempo. In fact, as one of his biographers wrote, he resembled the famous

> "... young lady of Rio
> Who played a Beethoven trio,
> But her technic was scanty,
> So she played it *Andante*
> Instead of *Allegro con brio*."

Johannes Brahms received numerous honors in his lifetime. Hamburg finally feted him with a "Brahms Evening" at which he played his Second Piano Concerto and the Rhapsodies for Piano. In 1895, he attended a three-day festival where his music was presented with that of Bach and Beethoven. He received an honorary degree from the University of Breslau. Cambridge offered one, but he turned it down because he did not wish to cross the English Channel.

Brahms also received tangible rewards for his efforts. He spent little on himself, but his generosity to others, including his family, knew no limits. He fed the birds, and he loved children; they called him "Onkel Brahms." Fireworks fascinated him, and books were often piled high on all his chairs. He once said, "So long as I have healthy legs and a good book, I can snap my fingers at the Universe."

Johannes Brahms hated to write letters and rejoiced when postcards were invented. Yet, he wrote well and possessed a keen sense of humor--he once suggested that his publisher come out with his "Lullaby" in a minor key for naughty and ailing children. He owned a trick rocking chair and delighted in luring unsuspecting guests into it. If they sat too near the edge, they were thrown to the floor; if they leaned too far back their legs went flying into the air.

The boy who started life as a thin, blue-eyed blond grew into a stocky, bearded man who smoked strong cigars and drank strong coffee. He hated dressing up and frequently wore the same clothes day in and day out. He once mended his trousers with sealing wax, and he often wore a shawl held together with a large safety pin. When he packed to go on tour, he assembled everything on a table and then tipped it into his trunk.

One characteristic never changed. Brahms arose at dawn and worked hard all his life. Being a perfectionist, he revised constantly, writing more for his wastebasket than for publication. His "Tricks"--as he modestly called his compositions--included four symphonies, two piano concertos, a violin concerto, chamber music, a requiem and other choral music, songs, and organ music. The piano music included sonatas, variations, intermezzi, fantasias, capriccios, waltzes, Hungarian dances, and rhapsodies. For Clara's children, he dreamed up *Fourteen Children's Folk Songs* with piano accompaniment. He also turned out some effective technical studies still in print.

When Brahms learned that his beloved Clara had suffered a stroke, he turned to composing *Four Serious Songs*. He completed them on his birthday, May 7, 1896. Thirteen days later, Clara died. Brahms left for Frankfurt upon hearing the news, but took the wrong train and arrived too late for the service. He continued on to Bonn, arriving in time for the burial--after a total of forty hours on the train.

Less than a month before his death the following April, Brahms attended a performance of his Fourth Symphony. The audience applauded wildly and called the composer to the front of his box even between movements. It was Vienna's final tribute.

16. THEODOR LESCHETIZKY

One of Brahms's friends was a piano teacher named Theodor Leschetizky. Three years older than Johannes, he started life in a romantic setting: a castle in Poland. Here, his father held a position as music master to a wealthy family. At the age of five, Theodor became one of his father's pupils, with the understanding that he must practice two hours each day.

Four years later, Theodor appeared in a public concert playing a Czerny concertino with an orchestra conducted by the son of Wolfgang Mozart. The old wooden hall in which the concert took place had been invaded by several families of rats. The child admitted being more concerned about the rats than about the music he played.

After the Leschetizkys moved to Vienna, Theodor began to study with Czerny. He met and became friendly with Chopin's most talented pupil, Karl Filtsch. But the greatest influence here came from the playing of Julius Schulhoff, who seemed to make the piano sing. Theodor studied counterpoint and sang in the choir until his voice changed.

At the age of fourteen, the young musician began to give lessons and play in public regularly. He performed in Russia, Austria, Germany, and England. After playing in the Michael Theatre in St. Petersburg, he received an invitation to play for the emperor, Nicholas I. When Anton Rubinstein left town to go on tour, Leschetizky took over for him, serving as concertmaster at the court of the grand duchess, sister of the emperor.

Theodor continued his own private teaching until, not unlike the old woman in the shoe, he had so many pupils he didn't know what to do. He decided to train assistants to prepare the less gifted. When the St. Petersburg Conservatory opened, Leschetizky started teaching there. Students arrived from all over Europe. A young girl named Annette Essipov began to study with him at the age of twelve. She possessed extraordinary talent, became an assistant and, eventually, his second wife.

When Leschetizky moved back to Vienna, he bought a house and decided to rest a while from teaching. But word got around, and the studio soon swarmed with students once more. He did save some time for composing, and when his second opera had its opening in Mannheim, he prepared to attend. His friend Franz Liszt arrived just as he was about to leave for the railroad station. In the excitement of this surprise visit, Leschetizky missed his train, the only one for the day.

The famous teacher enjoyed the simpler things in life: riding on the upper level of a London bus, going on sleigh rides, and taking long walks with his favorite pupils. He spent many summers in his attractive villa in the hills of Ischl. Johannes Brahms often rested on a bench kept in the garden here.

Leschetizky loved parties and welcomed any excuse for one. His Christmas celebrations always included music, specially selected gifts on a sparkling tree, dancing, and good food. He considered the seasoning of food an art and thought all girls should know how to prepare a meal.

A statue of Beethoven adorned his garden, and a marble bust of Chopin kept watch in his studio. He often said "Good Morning" or "Good-bye" to his piano by playing a chord. For the student, Leschetizky used a Bösendorfer, while *he* presided at a Beckstein. Both pianos were provided by the manufacturers. Lessons lasted about an hour, and the master taught from noon until four, with an occasional evening lesson.

Classes were given on Wednesday afternoons, starting at about five o'clock. In the beginning they were held weekly, for four or five hours and with a break for coffee. Later they became more formal affairs for which a fee was charged, sort of a dress rehearsal attended by up to two hundred people. Visiting artists such as Liszt or Rubinstein sometimes appeared on the program. Often, Leschetizky invited some of his pupils to stay for supper.

Their position at the table reflected his opinion of their performance for the class: the ones that had impressed him most sat closest to the teacher. A game of billiards usually followed the meal, lasting far into the night.

Leschetizky's energy knew no bounds. He possessed a magnetic personality and a generous heart. He was a marvelous mimic, as was Chopin. Being a stern taskmaster, he sometimes found it hard to "keep his cool." Unlike Liszt, who rarely lost his temper, Leschetizky could fuss and fume, even stalk angrily from the room. If lessons were an ordeal for an unprepared student, they were equally trying for the master. He once remarked, "Do you know, this life is really killing me. I suffer so in some of the lessons. I give my heart's blood. They say 'yes' but they play 'no.' "

Much of Leschetizky's advice applies universally. He particularly emphasized the need for listening when practicing: "The brain must guide the fingers, not the fingers the brain." "The fingers are nothing but little trained animals and know nothing themselves, so that everything depends on your direction." "Two hours, or three at most, is all anyone should require if he will only listen to what he is playing and criticize every note." "You can conquer the world with beautiful tones." "You don't need rules for the pedal--you need common sense and your ear to direct."

The teacher pricked the balloon flaunted by many piano students when he said, ". . . do not accustom yourselves to a first-rate piano. If you do, it will lead you to think you are responsible for the beautiful sounds that come out of it; whereas very likely it is but its natural tone--independent of your skill. At home you think: 'What a lovely touch I have.' Then you come to me. You play abominably, and say it is the fault of my piano. It is not my piano at all. It is you. Your hand is not under control, you have not learnt the principle of things. If you really know how to produce a certain effect --and produce it as the result of your knowledge, not of your piano--you can face almost any instrument with a clear conscience."

Leschetizky had many brilliant and well-known pianists as pupils, including Ignace Jan Paderewski. This famous pianist once said of his teacher, "The method of Leschetizky is very simple. His pupils learn to evoke a fine tone from the instrument and to make music and not noise. There are principles, you will agree, that are to be uniformly inculcated in every pupil --that is, breadth, softness of touch and precision in rhythm. For the rest, every individual is treated according to the nature of his talent."

Theodor Leschetizky died in 1915 at the age of eighty-five. He is remembered as one of the greatest piano teachers who ever lived.

Theodor Leschetizky (1830 - 1915)

17. EDVARD GRIEG

Edvard Grieg was another pianist to whom Johannes Brahms extended friendship. When the Norwegian composer gave his first concert in Vienna, Brahms sat on the platform with him. And though quite ill by now, he managed to attend the reception afterwards.

Born in Bergen, Norway, in 1843, Edvard first studied piano with his mother, an accomplished pianist who often played in public. The child particularly enjoyed experimenting with various harmonies, finding this more exciting than practicing the assigned scales.

Edvard found school equally uninteresting and soon devised an ingenious scheme to avoid regular attendance. Living over two miles from the schoolhouse, he frequently set out on foot in the morning downpour common in Bergen. He writes, "At school there was a rule that no boy who came late should be allowed into class but, as a punishment, should stand outside until the end of lessons. So if on one of these days of pouring rain I started off--as happened often--with none of my lessons prepared . . . I used also to go down the street and place myself under the rain spout of a house until I was wet to the skin. When at last I reached the classroom, such a stream of water would run from my clothes on to the floor that the master . . . would send me home immediately to change my clothes--which, on account of the long distance, was the same as letting me off morning school." Edvard made the mistake of arriving soaking wet when it had hardly rained at all and "a watch was set. One fine day I was caught and then I made a forcible acquaintance with 'percussion instruments.'"

Edvard made another mistake one day. He took to school a piece of manuscript on which there was the title (in capitals): "VARIATIONS ON A GERMAN MELODY FOR THE PIANO by Edvard Grieg, Opus 1." When the teacher discovered it, he called another instructor into the room saying, "Just look at this--that young scamp there is a composer." But the musician's triumph soon turned to chagrin. The German teacher grabbed him by the hair and announced emphatically, "Another time he will have the German dictionary with him as he should and leave such trash at home."

At the age of fifteen, on the recommendation of Norway's famous violinist, Ole Bull, Edvard entered the Leipzig Conservatory. Here, homesick at first, the boy finally started to apply the unbounded energy he had inherited from his mother. He may have carried a sound idea too far, for he developed pleurisy and one of his lungs collapsed. Much of the Leipzig instruction he found boring, but he particularly prized the piano lessons with Moscheles.

Of these lessons, Grieg said, "Often I had not played four bars before he would lay his hands over mine, push me gently off the stool and say, 'Now listen to what I make of it.' . . . I was initiated into many small technical secrets and learned to appreciate to the full his brilliant interpretations." He was exposed to Moscheles's 24 studies, Opus 70, also. After playing one of these "without once being stopped," he was rewarded by hearing Moscheles say, "See, gentlemen, that is musical piano playing."

Other highlights at Leipzig included hearing Clara Schumann perform her husband's concerto, listening to *Tannhäuser* "fourteen times running," and appearing on the Gewandhaus stage. In this first of several performances as soloist or conductor, Grieg played his own music: Opus 1. (On his sixtieth birthday, the placing of his bust in the foyer made him a permanent fixture at the Gewandhaus.)

Upon his return to Norway with piano pieces, songs, and a string quartet, Edvard gave a concert in Bergen. A year later, he went to Copenhagen to study. Here he met Rikard Nordraak, who wrote the music to the Norwegian National Anthem. This dynamic young composer stirred the fire of Grieg's innate love for things Norwegian:

folk music, fairy tales, and poetry. In addition, he inspired confidence in the shy, sensitive youth.

While in Denmark, Grieg became engaged to his cousin, Nina Hagerup. A musician who possessed an exceptional voice, she reported that the engagement followed their playing of Schumann's B-flat symphony as a duet. The parents objected. Nina's mother said, "He *is* nothing, *has* nothing, and writes music no one will listen to." But they were married and lived happily together. Edvard's mother knitted her "prayers and good wishes" into several pairs of socks for her son and contributed her grand piano to the new household.

Edvard spent eight years in the capital of Norway. He taught piano, conducted the Philharmonic Society, and founded the Norwegian Academy of Music. During summers, he escaped to the country to revel in composing and the lofty air. A nature lover, he once said that a mountain tour excited him much as would the "prospect of hearing Beethoven's 10th Symphony."

When visiting in Rome, Edvard met Liszt and played for him. Liszt sightread Grieg's Sonata for Violin, and the young composer laughed like a child. Liszt, it seemed, was all over the piano, bringing out the violin part even in the middle of the piano part. At the second meeting, the Abbé enthusiastically sightread his guest's Piano Concerto in A minor. It may have been Liszt's influence that won Grieg a yearly honorarium from Norway, permitting his return to Bergen.

When the Griegs decided to spend a winter in Loftus, Edvard needed a quiet place to compose. He had built, a short distance from the house where they were staying, "a square wooden box big enough for a piano, a fireplace and the master himself." Appropriately, he called the workshop "The Compost." He could work only in complete solitude. When he discovered a path leading to his door, he decided to move to another scenic spot.

Fifty townspeople arrived to help tear "The Compost" from its foundation--a feat accomplished with a "mighty tug" amidst "tumultuous shouts of applause." At the chosen sight, the movers were rewarded with a bulging barrel of ale and a festive spread of Norwegian delicacies "presided over by my worthy and amiable hostess, famed throughout

Hardanger for her beauty and intelligence. After the tourists found the new location, the hut was sold. It became a doll house.

When the composer built his dream house near Bergen, he called it "Troldhaugen," hill of sprites. It overlooks the Hardanger fjord. At the entrance, a post bears an inscription that reads, translated: "Edvard Grieg does not wish to receive callers earlier than four in the afternoon." Down the hill, nearer the water, is his "tune house." (Visitors can see his studio, complete with piano, just as the master left it. Even the two cushions, which he used because he was short, remain in the chair at his desk.)

Despite an ever-increasing problem with poor health, Grieg composed when he could and forced himself to make concert tours to many European cities. He conducted and played piano solos, chamber music, or accompaniments, often to his wife's dramatic singing. In 1889, he gave concerts in Paris, including one at Pleyel's. In London, he became a special favorite and played for Queen Victoria at Windsor Castle.

The composer refused all invitations to visit America because, not being well, he feared seasickness. He told one American that he would be glad to visit his country if he "could get a guarantee that the Atlantic would behave itself: but it must be a written guarantee."

Edvard Grieg found performing in public extremely painful. In one of his numerous letters he wrote, ". . .a public appearance is the most horrible thing I know. My nerves, my whole system, suffer indescribable tortures, but a certain something, I know not what, urges me on irresistibly. I cannot withstand a beautiful orchestral performance and a sympathetic audience. . . ."

Passionately fond of oysters, he wrote on another occasion that appearing in public caused such "colossal nervous excitement" that he preferred to avoid it "unless it enables me to demolish an unlimited amount of oysters."

His playing has been described as "tender" and "elegant," his technique as "flawless" and "smooth." A biographer, Henry T. Finck, called him "a veritable Orpheus on the piano."

On his way to England shortly before his death, Grieg had planned to conduct a concert at Leeds. His friend Percy Grainger, a young Australian and superb interpreter of his Northern music, was to perform his piano concerto. Only a short time before, Grieg had made a prophetic entry in his diary about Grainger. It read: "He is ⟵ , you are ⟶ ."

Edvard Grieg died September 4, 1907. On the day of his funeral, the boats in Bergen harbor flew flags at half mast. At 12 o'clock, all the church bells began to ring. About five hundred heard his music played and sung at the service held in the hall of the Westland Museum of Industrial Art. Thousands lined the streets to watch the procession. Nina walked behind the hearse, which was drawn by four horses. As they left the museum, a band played Chopin's funeral march--fitting tribute to the "Chopin of the North."

Edvard Grieg at work in "The Compost"

Edward MacDowell (1860-1908)

18. EDWARD MACDOWELL

Edvard Grieg was seventeen years old when Edward MacDowell was born in New York City. Except for the difference in age and nationality, they might have been twins. They composed the same kind of music, they had the same interests, and they were both modest and often dissatisfied with what they wrote. Both married musicians who were devoted helpmates, and each became the foremost composer in his country. The two never met, but because of mutual admiration, they became pen pals.

Edward MacDowell's active imagination revealed itself at an early age. He liked to write fairy tales, and from his father, he inherited a gift for drawing. Young Edward soon directed most of his attention toward the piano, although original sketches often decorated his music books.

Edward began lessons at the age of eight. As was the case with Grieg, he preferred composing to practicing. He received occasional piano lessons from a famous Venezuelan pianist, Teresa Carreño. In the spring of 1876, when the boy was fifteen, his mother took him to Paris. He passed the entrance exam for the Paris Conservatoire and studied piano, theory, and composition there. Later he transferred to Stuttgart and, finally, to Frankfurt for additional work in piano and composition.

When Edward's piano teacher retired from the Frankfurt Conservatory, he recommended his talented pupil as his successor, but MacDowell failed to receive the appointment because of his age. Only twenty-one, he was known as "the handsome American." He had deep blue eyes, a pink and white complexion, a reddish mustache, and jet black hair.

After being appointed to the position of head piano teacher at the

Darmstadt Conservatory, MacDowell moved there, but because he missed the excitement of the larger city, he soon returned to Frankfurt. In addition to traveling to Darmstadt, he went once a week to a medieval castle to teach young counts and countesses. They were not much interested in music: on occasion, the teacher looked up from the piano to find all his pupils sleeping with their heads upon their arms. He spent twelve hours a week on the train, using the time to read German and English poetry and to compose.

MacDowell became so flustered by an unexpected visit from his composition teacher, Joachim Raff, that he told him he'd been writing a concerto, which was not quite true. Herr Raff instructed him to bring it to him the following Sunday. MacDowell says, "I worked like a beaver. . . . Sunday came, and I only had the first movement composed. I wrote him a note making some wretched excuse, and he put it off until the Sunday after. Something happened then, and he put it off two days more; by that time I had the concerto ready."

Edward took his concerto to Weimar and played it for Liszt, who praised both music and playing. The Master arranged for MacDowell to appear at the Society of German Musicians' Convention in Zurich, where he performed his *First Piano Suite*. Surprised at the enthusiastic reception, he said that while "I would not have changed a note in one of them for untold gold . . . the idea that anyone else might take them seriously had never occurred to me." He had not even presumed to play the pieces from memory. This suite and the *Second Modern Suite*, published upon the recommendation of Liszt, were his first compositions to be printed.

MacDowell still regarded composition as a sort of sideline. In later years, he wrote, "I had acquired from early boyhood the idea that it was expected of me to become a pianist, and every moment spent in 'scribbling' seemed to be stolen from the more legitimate work of piano practice." He taught, played in concerts, and gradually devoted more and more time to composing. Friends who were conductors helped him with orchestration by trying out his scores with their orchestras.

At the age of twenty-three, MacDowell returned to America to marry a pupil, Marian Nevin. They honeymooned in London before going back to Frankfurt, where he spent much of his time composing, reading, and taking long walks with his bride. Recommended for two important posts, he was turned down for both, again because of his youth.

After moving to Wiesbaden, Edward completed his second piano concerto. One day while walking with a friend, he came upon a small ramshackle cottage squatting at the edge of the woods. It overlooked the town, with the Rhine and Main rivers in the distance. He decided immediately he had to have the place. After buying it, he worked in his garden, tramped through the woods, and composed industriously. He turned out symphonic poems, choral music, piano music, and many songs.

MacDowell's music was performed first in Europe. Then his name began to appear on concert programs in New York and Boston. Various pianists, including Teresa Carreño, introduced his music. When his first piano concerto was presented at Boston's Chickering Hall, the *Transcript* reviewer reported that, "The effect upon all was simply electric."

More and more Americans visited the Wiesbaden cottage. Some of them urged the MacDowells to return to their native land. Happy as they were in their scenic retreat, they felt that America promised greater financial reward. Reluctantly, they sold their house and moved to Mount Vernon Street in Boston.

Edward MacDowell was not quite twenty-eight when he made his American debut in a chamber music concert. The following spring, he played his second piano concerto in New York and then in Boston. Music and pianist received loud applause in both cities. That summer, he and his wife returned to Europe on vacation. MacDowell played the concerto in an "American Concert" at the Paris Exposition. When he performed it a few years later with The Philharmonic Society of New York, the *Evening Post* described "a success, both as pianist and composer, such as no American musician has ever won before a metropolitan concert audience," saying his ovation resembled that accorded "a popular prima donna at the opera."

Everywhere, audiences and critics received Edward MacDowell warmly. Aside from great speed--someone said he "took to prestissimo like a duck to water"--his playing showed great strength. He could start with a shadowy whisper and crescendo to a rousing *fortissimo*.

One of his pupils wrote: "He never approached the piano like a conqueror. He had a nervous way of saying that he didn't know whether things would go, because he had no time to practice." Yet "he would sit down and play ... with fingers dipped in lightning, fingers that flashed over the keys in perfect evenness and with perfect sureness."

MacDowell possessed an exceptional talent for teaching. At the age of thirty-five, he organized a music department for Columbia University, teaching all the courses himself the first two years. They included harmony, theory, composition, counterpoint, and orchestration, as well as piano. He taught methodically but with much imagination and originality. Students started arriving for his 9:30 a.m. classes an hour early so as to get seats close to the piano. "Someone at the window would say 'Here he comes!' and, entering the room with a huge bundle of music under his arm and his hat in his hand, MacDowell would deposit them on the piano and turn to us with a gracious smile." Then he would walk back and forth throwing out short, easily understood sentences in *vivace* tempo.

Except for a year's sabbatical when he toured the United States and visited the European Continent, MacDowell taught for eight years. He worked steadily at composition as well. He wrote many songs and his third and fourth piano sonatas, the "Norse" and the "Keltic," which he dedicated to Edvard Grieg.

Much of his composing was done in a log cabin he had built on a sixty-five-acre farm in Petersborough, New Hampshire. The couple spent their summers there, and MacDowell gained some of his inspiration from this picturesque spot with its view of Mount Manadnock. He loved to hike, fish, and as the natives said, "pretend to hunt." An excellent marksman, he was too tenderhearted to kill "without a pang."

Marian MacDowell, in her *Random Notes on Edward MacDowell and His Music*, relates anecdotes about two of the *Woodland Sketches*. Of "To a Wild Rose," she wrote that her husband tried to dream up at least one short theme each morning, which often wound up in the wastebasket. One day she happened to find a theme she thought ought not to be discarded. Edward admitted it wasn't bad, adding that it reminded him of the wild roses near his cabin. Of "To a Water-lily," Mrs. MacDowell wrote that while out riding in the buggy, they suddenly noticed a delightful perfume in the air. As they rounded a curve in the road, they discovered a dark pool bursting with water lilies.

Edward MacDowell, who published a book of poetry, set the mood for much of his music with bits of verse. Most of the titles are taken from his reading, his experiences, or from nature. Many of the themes for the *Second (Indian) Suite* for orchestra are from songs of the North American Indians. The *Sea Pieces* were suggested by his deep love for the ocean. Some, such as "From a Wandering Iceberg," stemmed from events occurring on his many crossings of the Atlantic.

After MacDowell resigned his position at Columbia, he continued with private teaching and composing. The next spring, he suffered what appeared to be a nervous breakdown. Even a summer in his favorite New Hampshire hills could not restore his health. It became apparent that his illness was more serious than at first suspected. Gradually, his brain tissues deteriorated, and he became like a young child, sitting at the window and dreaming or looking at a book of fairy tales.

MacDowell lingered for four years, dying at the age of forty-seven, five months after the death of his Norway "twin." He is buried near the log cabin used as a studio. A bronze tablet on a large boulder is inscribed with the lines he wrote for one of his *New England Idylls*, "From a Log Cabin":

> A house of dreams untold
> It looks out over the whispering tree tops
> And faces the setting sun.

Edward MacDowell left two memorials. The first includes sixty-two opus numbers, representing nearly two hundred separate compositions. The second, the MacDowell Colony, is the result of dedicated effort on the part of Marian MacDowell, who died in 1956 at the age of ninety-eight.

Like Clara Schumann, Mrs. MacDowell gave numerous concerts of her husband's music. She donated the proceeds as well as the Petersborough Farm to a memorial association to establish a retreat for composers, artists, writers, and photographers.

Thirty-six cabins were built. Some are equipped with fireplaces, porches, and indoor plumbing. All are blessed with privacy and freedom from the distractions of humdrum routine. Each noon, basket lunches appear outside the door as if by magic. Evening meals can be taken in a community dining room and are often followed by programs that demonstrate the accomplishments of those in residence.

Each cabin contains a "guest book." Colonists may carve their names on flat pieces of wood called "tombstones." Engravings such as "Leonard Bernstein," "Aaron Copland," "Sara Teasdale," and "Thornton Wilder" make witness to the fact that the MacDowell Colony embraces all the arts. It forms a fitting and far-reaching memorial, in tune with the talents of Edward MacDowell.

19. CLAUDE DEBUSSY

While studying at the Paris Conservatoire, Edward MacDowell met a slightly younger student named Achille. The boy signed his name as "Ach. de Bussy," then "Claude Debussy." When he grew up, his signature became "Claude Debussy, musicien français."

Achille-Claude Debussy made his entrance onto this world's stage in 1862. His mother and father operated a china shop at Saint-Germain-en-Laye, just outside Paris. When their eldest son was two years old, the family gave up their shop and moved to Clichy and then to Paris. Achille received no more than meager schooling. What music he heard consisted of the popular melodies of the day and the band concerts played in the Paris parks. On special occasions, he was taken to the theatre or the opera by his father, who liked music.

The boy showed interest in painting, collected brilliantly colored butterflies, and decorated his room with pictures or other ornaments. When he began to visit regularly in Cannes, Achille developed a passion for the sea. His father decided he should become a sailor.

While at the seashore, Achille acquired another interest. He had his first piano lessons and delighted in trying out chords on an old battered piano. He heard a Norwegian carpenter who "sang from morning till night." Years later, he said "perhaps the songs were Grieg's." After he played for a lady who claimed to have studied with Chopin, she gave him a few lessons and announced he should become a musician. From then on, his father forced the lad to work six or eight hours a day at the newly chosen profession.

At the age of eleven, Achille Debussy went for his first class at the Paris Conservatoire, wearing a red-tasseled sailor's cap. (Later he came to prefer cowboy hats.) Out of thirty-eight candidates, he was one of eight to pass the entrance examination. He had the problems of most gifted children in conforming to the regulations of an institution as strict as the Conservatoire. But the young professor of solfège recognized his talent, and the two often spent hours after class studying scores such as Wagner's *Tannhäuser.* On one occasion, they became so engrossed that they forgot about the time and were locked in the building.

The other teachers were not as impressed, nor did his classmates take any special notice of him. One member of Marmontel's piano class later mentioned that Achille was small in size and often late for class. His only outstanding feature seemed to have been his forehead. He was also one of the youngest in the class, although certainly not the best. The same student mentioned his habit of emphasizing strong beats of the measures with a loud puff or a sort of hiccup.

Another referred to his "weird playing," saying "he used literally to throw himself on the keyboard and exaggerate every effect. He seemed to be in a violent rage with the instrument...." But occasionally, he gave a glimpse of things to come by producing "marvelously soft and delicate effects."

When not quite twelve, Achille won the second honorable mention in the advanced piano competition, playing Chopin's second piano concerto. At the age of fourteen, he won the second prize with a performance of the first movement of Robert Schumann's Sonata in G minor. Other awards were won in solfège, sightreading, and harmony.

For four summers, young Debussy was exposed to a world entirely different from the one in which he grew up. The first summer, he served as a pianist in a chateau that had once been the residence of Catherine de' Medici. Here, he replaced a Conservatory friend named José-Manuel Imenez. One of his duties consisted of playing the piano until the lady of the house, an insomniac, finally fell prey to the sandman.

The next three summers, Achille was employed by Tchaikovsky's famous benefactor, Madame von Meck. He played duets with her and gave lessons to and accompanied her eleven children. He played in a trio with a violinist and cellist, and was introduced to music of Borodin, Rimsky-Korsakov, and

Balakirev, as well as that sung by gypsies in the Moscow cabarets. Part of the time he spent traveling to Vienna and to Italy. Madame von Meck described him as being easy to please and always good-natured. She also appreciated his sense of humor and talent for mimicry, which she said everyone found entertaining.

During the winters, Debussy spent much of his time at the home of an elderly architect and his beautiful young wife. The couple and their friends were well-educated, and the young musician tried to make up for his own shortcomings by reading numerous books, including an encyclopedia. He gave lessons to the couple's daughter, who described the eighteen-year-old teacher as "a big, beardless boy, with strong marked features and thick, black, curly hair, which he wore flat on his forehead. But in the evening, when his hair had become untidy--which suited him much better--my parents used to say that he looked like some medieval Florentine type." For five years, he did most of his composing in this house. The Vasniers' daughter also said: "He would improvise for a long time, then walk up and down humming, with the everlasting cigarette in his mouth, or else rolling tobacco and paper in his fingers. When he had found what he wanted, he began to write."

At the age of twenty-two, Debussy won the Grand Prix de Rome awarded by the Academy of Fine Arts, for his composition *L'Enfant prodigue*. This required him to leave the Vasnier home and, perhaps because of the separation, he felt no enthusiasm for the honor. Nicknamed "the Prince of Darkness," he spent only two years at the Villa Medici, although he was entitled to three years there. Much of the music he wrote here was received coolly by the Academy. He did have the pleasure of meeting Liszt and hearing him play. What he recalled thirty years later about this event was Liszt's skillful use of the pedal.

Recognition crept toward Claude Debussy at a snail's tempo, *larghissimo*. He conducted a chorus; taught piano, voice, harmony, drama; took various jobs as accompanist; and he composed. At one time, he lived in a sparsely furnished attic room with only an old broken-down table, three straight-back chairs, and a bed; but he had an elegant Pleyel piano on loan.

In the early days, the problem of earning a living was a constant one. He once spent his last cent on a porcelain cat he saw in a window on his way to buy food. (Particularly fond of live gray angora cats, he owned several, one at a time. He named them all "Line.") On the morning of his first marriage, Debussy was forced to give a piano lesson in order to pay for the wedding breakfast.

The first appreciation of the musician's abilities came from his friends, most of whom were artists or writers. Debussy was in his early thirties before he received any public notice. This notice was first brought about through his opera *Pelléas and Mélisande*, which he had worked on for ten years. Presented at the Opéra Comique with Mary Garden singing the lead, it gradually worked its way into the hearts of a few musicians, critics, and the general public. By now, the composer himself was reviewing operas and concerts, eventually becoming a critic for a Paris daily. Seven or eight years later, he was honored by an appointment to the Supreme Council of the Musical Section of the Conservatoire.

Except for times when, as he said, his "brain was blind," Claude Debussy worked constantly at composing. Although his works were not without roots in the past, he was an innovator. Perhaps he had found, smoldering in some salon or at Pleyel's, a spark from the fire of Chopin's talent. Freeing it from the ash, he carried it outdoors to light his own fire--much as the Impressionists had taken painting out of the studio into the open air. He broke the constraints of scales, chords, and musical form by raising or lowering the fifth of diatonic scales and using church modes, five-tone or whole-tone scales, or scales of folk music. He left so-called dissonant chords unresolved.

"I should like," Debussy wrote, "to see the creation ... of a kind of music free from themes and motives, or formed on a single continuous theme, which nothing interrupts and which never returns on itself. Then there will be a logical, compact, deductive development." Sometimes the music seems to float in space, suggesting an Impressionistic painting or delicate fine lace. But it can be joyful or humorous, as well.

Debussy's subjects were as varied as his treatment of them. He musically painted whatever he saw or heard that impressed him; inspiration came from poetry, paintings, the sky or sea, from the cabarets and music halls.

A favorite haunt was the *Chat Noir* in Montmartre. Another spot frequented by Debussy and Toulouse Lautrec was called Reynold's. Both men were enchanted by a couple of clowns who often dropped in there after an evening's performance at the circus. One made drawings of Chocolat and

Footitt, the other expressed his childlike love for the circus in his music.

The Paris Exposition of 1889 offered another source of inspiration. Debussy visited frequently with his friends, often hearing the improvisation of "liberated" musicians. Or he listened to small orchestras from Spain, China, Java, and other foreign lands as they played their native music.

The Sirens that sang the loudest were those of the sea. It was Debussy's first love. The waves, the sound of their lapping shore, the shimmer of sunlight on the water, or the vastness of the ocean: these all affected this sensitive man who was poet, painter, writer, and musician. He described the sea as "the one thing in Nature that puts you in your place; only one does not sufficiently respect the sea. To wet in it bodies deformed by the daily life should not be allowed."

Monsieur Debussy applied his ideas to orchestral and choral music, opera, chamber music, ballet, and a wealth of piano music. In the *Children's Corner Suite* dedicated to his daughter, "my dear little Chouchou," he showed love for "the little ones" and a sense of humor. The "Gradus ad Parnassum," with its bow to Clementi, he called "a kind of progressive, hygienic, gymnastic exercise to be played every morning, beginning *moderato* and working up gradually to an *animato*." "Jimbo's Lullaby" was written for Chouchou's toy elephant. "Golliwog's Cake Walk" imitates the music that preceded jazz, and it mimics Wagner's *Tristan and Isolde* in a section marked "with a great emotion."

Not one to be frightened by anything new, Debussy did rear back when confronted by the president of the Boston Orchestral Club. Mrs. Elisa Hall, who had taken up the saxophone for her health, commissioned the composer to write something for her instrument. Knowing little about the saxophone, he kept putting off the ordeal. One day he wrote a friend: "The Americans are proverbially tenacious. The Saxophone lady landed in Paris at 58 rue Cardinet . . . and is inquiring about her piece." To another friend he confessed, "Considering that this 'Fantasie" was ordered, and paid for, and eaten more than a year ago, I realize that I am behindhand with it. . . ." Adding to his procrastination was the sight of this lady in a pink frock playing on such an ungainly instrument." He eventually sent her a rough draft with blank measures and incomplete "bridges." The final edition was completed after his death by Roger-Ducasse.

As his fame spread, Debussy received invitations to appear as conductor or soloist in his own compositions. Although he possessed little talent for conducting and, consequently did not enjoy it, these appearances helped him to pay his bills. He traveled to such places as London, Rome, Brussels, Amsterdam, and Budapest. Serge Koussevitsky engaged him to conduct concerts in Moscow and St. Petersburg. In Oslo, the applause was led by Edvard Grieg, a composer for whom Debussy had much regard. Conducting in Vienna, Debussy had to rely upon an interpreter. "I sang, I gesticulated like a character in an Italian pantomine . . . it was enough to move the hardest heart."

While speaking of Debussy, a well-known composer-critic said that "art can never be what it was before he came." The same could be said for what happened when Debussy sat down at the piano. He introduced new pedal effects and quadruple pianissimos. He was criticized sometimes for playing too softly, as was Chopin.

Describing the magic of Debussy's playing, one writer said, "The sounds seem to be produced without any impact of hammers or vibration of strings; they rise up into a transparent atmosphere where they unite without merging, and then dissolve in iridescent mists. M. Debussy puts the keyboard under a spell, the secret of which is unknown to any of our virtuosi."

Depressed by World War I and its horrors, the musician seemed to have been deserted by the Muse. He was unable to write music. Finally he realized the futility of inactivity and went to work at "creating . . . a little of that beauty which the enemy is attacking with such fury." He wrote sonatas for various instruments and, for the piano, etudes dedicated to the memory of Chopin. He admitted some of the studies would "terrify your fingers," but said they "conceal their severe technical aspect beneath flowers of harmony--you don't catch flies with vinegar."

Many of his final concerts were frightful experiences for Debussy. He refused to give up, waging a gallant fight against serious medical problems that were finally diagnosed as cancer.

Debussy died in March of 1918. Paris was still under attack, and the thunder of guns rumbled in the distance. The skies were cloudy and only a few mourners ventured out. The minister of education led the procession followed by the conductors of the two symphonic societies. Few pedestrians or shopkeepers paid attention to the event. But those who noticed the ribbons on the wreaths realized they were for "some musician."

If he could have spoken, Debussy might have said, as he once told a Viennese critic, "I am I." And he might have added with justifiable pride, "Claude Debussy, musicien français."

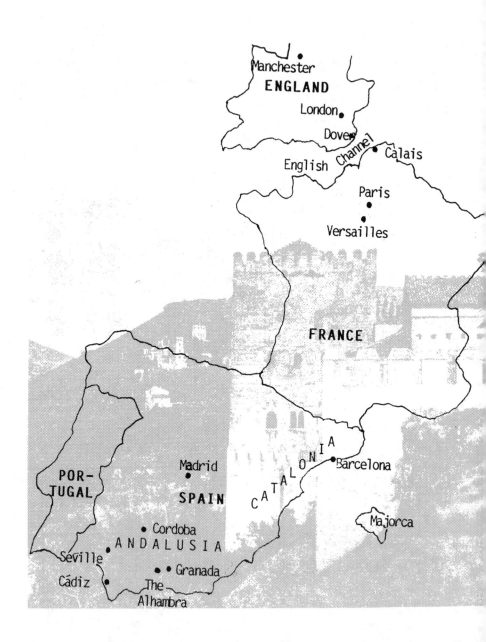

Spain with the Alhambra in background

20. ALBENIZ, GRANADOS, and FALLA

Spanish music is a mosaic of moods and colors: fiery spangled reds, dreamy romantic blues, somber melancholy grays. Spain itself is a land of contrasts, with snowy mountains and sandy beaches, cathedrals and fortresses, religious pageants and fighting bulls. Phoenicians, Greeks, Carthaginians, Romans, Visigoths, Arabs, Moors and Christians have all lived in Spain. With the gypsies in the south (Andalusia), they have all added color with songs and dances, guitars, tambourines, and castanets.

Organs and harpsichords were popular there, but another keyboard instrument had been dozing backstage since the 1740's. While Domenico Scarlatti was writing hundreds of harpsichord sonatas, the Spanish court owned five pianos. But, as was the case with Johann Sebastian Bach, Scarlatti did not take any particular interest in the newfangled fortepiano--nor did most of his successors.

In 1860, Isaac Albéniz was born in northeastern Spain, not far from Barcelona. He was a child prodigy with an older sister, as was Wolfgang Mozart. Isaac's sister became his first piano teacher. His father also took an interest in his talent, forcing him to practice long hours.

At the age of four, Isaac gave his first public concert. When he was six years old, he went to Paris with his mother. For nine months, he studied with Marmontel, who would later teach MacDowell and Debussy. He supposedly passed entrance exams for the Conservatoire but was told to return in two years.

In the meantime, the family moved to Madrid, and Isaac enrolled at the conservatory there. His father arranged numerous tours, showing off the lad and his sister in concerts. For these performances, the "artist," Isaac, dressed in the costume of a French musketeer, complete with sword.

Soon bored with life--he'd been reading Jules Verne--Isaac began running away from home. On his own, he toured northern Spain, giving concerts and making money, part of which was stolen by highway robbers. After his sister died, he returned home.

Once more bitten by the wanderlust bug, the young pianist then headed south. Threatened with arrest, he stowed away on a ship bound for Panama. He was twelve years old. Although he entertained passengers by playing for them, he was still put ashore at the first port, Buenos Aires. He became one of the "street people," sleeping outdoors and not eating regularly. Finally, he organized a concert tour and once more traveled the road to success. His father caught up with him in Cuba but finally agreed that he could go to the United States.

In New York, the youth worked as a porter on the docks and played piano in some waterfront bars. Eventually, he figured a way to play with the backs of his hands while seated back to the piano. With proceeds from concerts that included this trick, he crossed the country to San Francisco. Soon back in Europe, he stopped in England before going to Germany to study at Leipzig.

His pockets empty once again, Isaac returned to Spain to look for a patron. With the help of a grant from the king, he entered Brussels Conservatory at the age of fifteen. Still restless, he left again for America. Returning to Brussels, he won first prize for his piano playing. After an audition with Liszt, he took lessons from him in Weimar and in Rome.

Called the "Spanish Rubinstein," Isaac Albéniz toured Europe and America. In 1883 he married a pupil. He also signed up for composition lessons with Felipe Pedrell. This famous teacher introduced his pupils to the rich heritage of Spanish folk music.

Albéniz began to write what has been called "postcard music." Though born in Catalonia, he insisted he was a "Moor." His heart, he said, belonged to the Alhambra, that walled citadel completed in the fourteenth century by Mohammed I. Overlooking the city of Granada, part of the palace still remains. (The court of Lions and Court of the Myrtles are popular tourist attractions.)

Hundreds of piano pieces include numerous tributes to Andalusian folk music. Among them are *Sevilla, Granada, Cadiz,* and *Cordoba* (with its haunting melody and guitar-like accompaniment.)

After moving to Paris, Albéniz became friendly with Chausson, Fauré, Dukas, and d'Indy. He taught piano at the Schola Cantorum and dabbled in opera. Perhaps inspired by his French friends, he decided to tackle something more complicated. His final contribution to piano literature is called *Iberia.* It consists of four books of three pieces each. They celebrate Spain, its joy and its melancholy. Dozens of lively dance rhythms alternate with slower song-like sections called *copla.* All these pieces are extremely difficult-- they've been called "horrific." The talented pianist Blanche Selma looked at a manuscript and told the composer, "It is unplayable." Albéniz assured her, "You will play it." And she did. Debussy admired the work and spoke of its "jingling tambourines" and "colorful impressions."

Iberia was the swan song of Isaac Albéniz. His travels came to an end in the Basse-Pyranees when he was forty-nine years old. He was buried in Barcelona.

*   *   *

Enrique Granados, seven years younger than Isaac Albéniz, was also born in Catalonia. He studied first with his local bandmaster and then with a teacher in Barcelona. He applied for admission to the Paris Conservatoire but became ill and passed the age limit before recovering, so he took private lessons from one of the professors there. At the age of twenty-two, he settled in Barcelona, where he gave piano lessons and studied composition with Pedrell. He gave concerts in Spain and France and, in 1892, married a Spanish señorita.

Granados fell in love with the world of the Spanish painter Goya. Ladies and gentlemen of Madrid's high society adorned the walls of The Prado, national museum of painting and sculpture. Granados made sketches and wrote music inspired by them. The Granados masterpiece for the piano is the suite *Goyescas.* (He later wrote an opera on the same subject.) As does *Iberia, Goyescas* requires diligent practice. Harold Schonberg states that Alicia de Larrocha "tosses" it off as though it were "basic Czerny." Ernest Newman calls it a "gorgeous treat for the fingers. . . . fortepiano music of the purest kind."

Granados disliked traveling, especially on the water. He dreaded even the six- or seven-hour trip from Barcelona to Majorca. When asked what he'd do if invited to play a concert in America, he insisted he would not accept. But when his opera *Goyescas* was premiered by the Metropolitan Opera, he and his wife crossed the ocean for the occasion. On the return to Spain in March of 1916, his ship, the *Sussex*, was torpedoed and sunk by a German submarine. Like Albéniz, Granados was forty-nine years old when he died.

*   *   *

Manuel de Falla was born in Andalusia in 1876 in the seaport city of Cadiz. His mother, an accomplished pianist, gave her son his first lessons. Quiet, deeply religious, and not too healthy, he was blessed with an extra dollop of determination. He attended symphony concerts in the local museum and decided to become a composer. After hearing Grieg's work, he resolved to do for Spain what the older composer had done for Norway.

At the age of ten, Manuel was taken to Seville. He fell in love with the city and begged his family to move there. Failing in this, he invented his own imaginary city and called it *Colon* (Castilian for Columbus). The theatre of this "city" produced the child's first opera. As did Mendelssohn, Manuel published a magazine, writing and illustrating it. In the boy's mind, there were self-propelled vehicles similar to automobiles, which had not yet been invented.

When he was fourteen, Manuel de Falla gave his first public concert, which included his own compositions. He studied in Madrid with a pupil of a pupil of Chopin, José Tragó. After his father's business failed, the family moved to Madrid. When Pedrell also arrived in this city, Manuel took lessons in composition from him. In two years, he completed the seven-year conservatory course.

In July of 1904, the Academia de las Bellas Artes of Madrid announced a contest for a one-act Spanish opera. At about the same time, a piano contest was announced with a grand piano as the prize. Works to be played included a Bach fugue; a Beethoven sonata; and works of Schumann, Chopin, and others. The piano competition began on April 1, and the opera contest ended at sunset the night before. After working frantically to learn the pieces and compose the opera, Falla delivered the completed opera on March 31 and won the grand piano the following day. His opera, *La Vida Breve* (Life is Short), also won.

Following in the steps of his predecessors, Falla went to Paris. Dukas introduced him to Albéniz, and he met Debussy and Ravel. All were impressed with his talent. They spoke to the French music publisher Durand, who offered three hundred francs for Falla's *Four Spanish Pieces for Piano*. Debussy complained that this was fifty francs more than he'd been given for his quartet; Dukas said it was what he was paid for the *Sorcerer's Apprentice*; Albéniz announced he was paid nothing for his score of *Catalonia*; Ravel topped them all when he admitted Durand wouldn't take his quartet even as a gift.

Manuel de Falla flourished in Paris. Wearing a bowler hat and velvet-collared overcoat, he cut a fine figure. He met prominent artists, including the Russian Diaghilev, who later produced his *Three-Cornered Hat*. Publishers knocked on his door. He worked hard at composing, and he toured Europe as a concert pianist. In London, he introduced his *Four Spanish Pieces* dedicated to Albéniz.

When World War I broke out, Falla returned to Madrid. He completed *Nights in the Gardens of Spain*, a work for piano and orchestra, and a gypsy ballet. *Fastasia Bética* (Andalusian Fantasy) is the most difficult of Falla's piano compositions. A sort of summary of his music, it uses Phrygian and Aeolian modes, percussive guitar-like strumming, and Spanish dance rhythms.

Falla wrote a puppet opera for the private marionette theatre of a Paris princess. Based on an episode from Don Quixote, it was called *El Retablo de Maese Pedro* (Master Peter's Puppet Show). It was first produced in America by the League of Composers, using giant puppets. Wanda Landowska played the harpsichord part.

In 1922, Falla moved to Granada, which he considered the world's most beautiful city. His house, near the Alhambra, looked down on the city below, with the mountains in the distance. Fragrance from the nearby gardens perfumed the evening air, while gypsy songs and guitars added to the magic.

The following year, Falla began to work on a concerto for harpsichord, flute, oboe, clarinet, violin, and cello. He dedicated it to Landowska, who played it in Barcelona with Falla conducting. The press showed little enthusiasm. When the concerto was performed in Paris, Falla suddenly took over the harpsichord part himself, although Landowska's name appeared on the program. The reception this time proved spectacular.

The Spanish Civil War disturbed the nonviolent, peace-loving Manuel de Falla. Friends were arrested, and families broken up. Always generous to the poor, he gave money to a woman suspected of being a communist. When the authorities asked why, he replied, "Because I am baptized." Constantly campaigning for peace, he placed "PAZ" (Peace) at the head of all his letters.

When his good friend, the poet Lorca, was arrested and shot, Falla collapsed. He mended slowly, finally recovering enough to travel to Argentina to conduct a few concerts. He remained there for seven years, pathetically homesick and failing in health.

Nine days before his seventieth birthday, Manuel de Falla died of a heart attack. He is buried in the Cathedral of Cadiz beneath a slab of Granada marble. An inscription reads: "To God Alone Honor and Glory."

21. BÉLA BARTÓK

When Béla Bartók discovered the music of Claude Debussy, he realized immediately that he had found a kindred spirit. Although their use of the modes and scales of folk music took different directions, Bartók revered the older musician all his life and dedicated one of his *Improvisations* to the memory of Debussy. He frequently programmed Debussy's music in recitals and was called its greatest living interpreter by at least one critic.

Twenty years younger than the French composer, Béla Bartók was born in 1881 in a part of Hungary that now belongs to Rumania. His father directed the town's agricultural school, wrote articles for a journal he founded, and played the piano and cello. One day, the year-and-a-half-old boy became interested in a piece his mother played. The following day, he dragged her to the piano and kept shaking his head until she played the music noticed the day before. At the age of three, Béla received a drum on which he managed to beat out difficult rhythms as they were played. At four, he could play forty or more songs on the piano--with one finger.

Béla's mother started giving him piano lessons on his fifth birthday. She had trouble making him count since he felt rhythms instinctively. Instruction soon came to an end because of so much illness in the family, either that of the pupil or of the father. Béla suffered from a form of eczema and from frequent bouts with bronchitis. His mother writes that it upset him to constantly hear "Poor little Béla." Since "he could not play with the other children (because of the eruptions on his skin) it is no wonder that he became a quiet, serious child. Whenever he was ill and had to lie in bed, he always wanted me to sing and tell him stories. . . ."

When the boy heard a performance of his father's orchestra in a restaurant, he put down his fork and listened to the music. "How," he asked, "can all the others eat when such beautiful music is being played?"

After piano lessons were finally resumed, it became obvious that Béla possessed absolute pitch. He also showed an inclination toward composing, asking his mother to notate pieces for him. The child was eight when his father died. From then on, Mrs. Bartók supported her son and his sister Elza by teaching school and giving piano lessons.

At the age of eleven, Béla performed in public for the first time. He played the Allegro of the Beethoven *Waldstein Sonata* and one of his own compositions he had titled *The Danube River*. The audience applauded enthusiastically, and the soloist received seven bouquets, including one made of candy.

After the family moved to a larger city, Béla began to receive professional training in music. He heard orchestra concerts and operas and became friends with Erno Dohnányi, who was four years older. When Dohnányi left for Budapest's Royal Academy of Music, his young friend replaced him as organist in the Gymnasium chapel. Béla began to play in public, taught piano, and served as accompanist to a cellist. Some of the money earned went for orchestral scores: Brahms's, then Richard Strauss's and Liszt's.

At eighteen, Béla Bartók entered the Academy in Budapest, passing the entrance exam easily although he had been ill and unable to practice all summer. His piano teacher, István Thomán, had been a pupil of Liszt. Receiving little encouragement from the composition instructor, Béla concentrated on the piano and soon made a name for himself. After his first appearance at an Academy recital, a critic spoke of his "steely, well-developed technique," adding that the "young man has acquired extraordinary strength. A year and a half ago, his constitution was so weak that the doctors sent him to Merano lest the cold winter harm him--and now he plays the piano as thunderously as a little Jupiter." On the December 14, 1901, he gave a concert for which he received ten gold pieces. These he put into a coin purse and placed on the Christmas tree for his mother.

During his third year at the Academy, Bartók heard Strauss's "*Thus Spake Zarathustra*." He wrote ". . . I was aroused as by a flash of lightning . . . and began again to compose." After leaving school, he studied for a summer with Dohnányi before setting out to perform in such cities as Vienna, Berlin, and Manchester, England.

When he happened to hear a servant singing a melody handed down from Hungarian ancestors, Béla Bartók became interested in the music of his native land. He spent many summers in the country listening to and recording on an Edison phonograph the folk songs of the peasants. With the help of another Hungarian, Zoltán Kodály, he eventually notated, classified, and published over six thousand of them. He included songs of Turks and North African Arabs, as well as those of Hungarians and people of neighboring areas. A butterfly collector, he often carried with him a camera and a flask of alcohol in which to preserve any prize captured as it flitted by. Although he sometimes slept on "makeshift beds on benches" in schoolhouses, he frequently spoke of his days among the peasants as the happiest of his life.

At the age of twenty-six, Béla Bartók received an appointment as piano teacher at the Royal Academy, remaining there for nearly thirty years. One of his first pupils was a fourteen-year-old girl whom he married two years later. In addition to teaching and composing, he wrote many books and articles on folk music and published his autobiography.

Bartók gave concerts all over Europe. In Berlin, he met Fritz Kreisler. In Paris, he enjoyed the work of Impressionists in the Louvre saying, as had Chopin, that he felt he was listening to music when he looked at certain paintings. In London, he met American composer Henry Cowell, who introduced him to "tone clusters." He made tours of Spain, Portugal, Switzerland, and Russia. His son Béla wrote that his father's return from these trips was ". . . always a great pleasure for him and for us. He would come back laden with frozen reindeer meat, grapefruits, photographs, and all sorts of other gifts."

Bartók's Muse, like Debussy's, was silenced by the guns of war. But in 1915, he wrote a friend, "I have even found the time--and ability--to do some composing." His opera, *Bluebeard's Castle*, and a ballet, *The Wooden Prince*, gave him his first taste of public approval and helped him find a publisher.

Many young people were fans, but Hungarian critics remained lukewarm long after Bartók received recognition in other parts of Europe. One reviewer wrote of a performance of the *Four Orchestral Pieces* that "his work had the same effect upon us as if it had been played from back to front."

The opening concert of the first International Festival in Salzburg presented Bartók's first violin sonata. Succeeding festival programs often bore his name, frequently as composer and performer. His fortieth birthday was celebrated throughout Europe.

In 1927, Béla Bartók made a tour of the United States. Unfortunately, he found this country more interesting than it found him. From California he wrote, "Here I am on the shore of an ocean ... in a private wooden house on the ocean beach. The Pacific murmurs and rages noisily, and sometimes at night even shakes my bed. ..." No big waves billowed about his music, although a year later, his Third Quartet shared first prize and won six thousand dollars in the competition sponsored by Philadelphia's Musical Fund Society.

In 1940, war having broken out once more and his mother having died the year before, Béla Bartók decided to come again to the United States. He and his second wife, who had also been a pupil, gave a farewell concert in Budapest, each playing concertos. Of the performance he wrote, "... she played very beautifully--afterwards we played the Mozart 2-piano concerto and finally I played from the *Mikrokosmos*."

The couple arrived in the United States "without a change of clothes, without either a tuxedo or evening dress." Their luggage had been detained in Spain. Soon after their arrival in New York, they gave a Town Hall recital in which they performed the composer's *Sonata for Two Pianos and Percussion*. Two weeks later, in the same hall, they played Mozart, Debussy, Brahms, Bach, and Bartók. Later, they toured the country, taking bows in St. Louis, Denver, San Francisco, Seattle, Kansas City, and Detroit.

Bartók received an honorary doctorate from Columbia University. In conferring the degree, Dr. Nicholas Murray Butler called the composer a "distinguished teacher and master; internationally recognized authority on the folk music of Hungary, Slovakia, Romania, and Arabia ... a truly outstanding artist who has brought high distinction to the spiritual life of this country." Columbia also provided a part-time research position for him.

Concerts were given only occasionally. Of a two-piano recital in Chicago, Bartók wrote to a former pupil: "We played rather well, and got very bad criticisms ... as bad as I never got in my life. Just as if we were the last of the last pianists." The same letter bemoans the fact that one of their free pianos, "the upright one," was to be taken from them.

In 1943, the Bartóks were soloists in the first performance of the *Concerto for Two Pianos and Orchestra* with the New York Philharmonic. The audience applauded warmly, but the critics were cool. This concert brought Béla Bartók's career as a pianist to an end.

Lack of acceptance depressed the sensitive, talented musician. Lack of income accented the unhappy situation. He had never weighed over 116 pounds. As one conductor said, "Whoever met Bartók thinking of the rhythmic strength of his work was surprised by his slight, delicate figure."

From Asheville, North Carolina, where he had been sent for the winter under the sponsorship of ASCAP (America Society of Composers, Authors, and Publishers), Bartók wrote, "In March my weight was 87 pounds; now it is 105. I grow fat. I bulge....You will not recognize me."

In Asheville, the composer was able to complete the *Concerto for Orchestra.* He had been in the hospital when that friend of struggling, talented musicians, Serge Koussevitzky, appeared with a commission for his work. Bartók sat in the audience while the Boston Symphony "scored a major success" with its performance. A few days earlier, he heard Yehudi Menuhin play his *Sonata for Solo Violin* at a New York concert and was called to the stage to acknowledge the applause.

Bartók spent his last summer at Saranac Lake in New York, where he enjoyed being outdoors and watching the "chickmucks." Still scientifically minded, he applied himself to the problem of estimating the number of vibrations per second of the hummingbird's wings. (The answer, he concluded, was ninety to one hundred.) His son Peter joined him and helped by drawing the bar lines for the Third Piano Concerto, dedicated to the composer's wife, Ditta. He completed all but the last thirteen measures, writing the prophetic word "vege," a Hungarian expression meaning "end," at the bottom of his sketch copy. Béla Bartók died of leukemia at New York's West Side Hospital on September 26, 1945.

Almost immediately, Bartók's music burgeoned in concert halls and on recordings. He himself had recorded *Contrasts*, a rhapsody for violin, clarinet, and piano, with the artists for whom it was written: Joseph Szigeti and Benny Goodman.

The *Mikrokosmos*, a modern *Gradus ad Parnassum*, is a collection of 153 short pieces written originally for son Peter, who says they advanced more quickly than he did. They expose the student to many scales or modes and sometimes lead unsuspecting parents to ask from a distance, "Are you *sure* you're playing the right note?" It is a hauntingly beautiful introduction to twentieth-century music. Bartók also wrote *For Children*, based on Hungarian and Slovakian folk songs, some of them familiar to children everywhere.

As a pianist, Béla Bartók can be ranked with the immortals. A critic called him "one of the greatest and at the same time most poetic musical personalities of our times. . . . we have never heard more definitely outlined phrases, strong rhythms and cleaner tones than in the playing of Bartók."

That this basically frail human being managed such colossal contributions in so many fields may be due to the philosophy he expressed in his youth: "Each must strive to soar above all; nothing must touch him; he must be completely independent. Only thus can he reconcile himself to death and purposelessness. . . ."

To this, Bartók added prophetically, "It takes an enormous struggle to soar above everything!"

Originally buried in the United States, Bartók's wish to be interred in his native Hungary was finally granted. His remains were returned to Budapest in 1988. On July 7, more than ten thousand people filed past his coffin in the Academy of Science Building to the strains of the composer's now famous *Concerto for Orchestra*.

Béla Bartók (1881-1945)

Prokofiev's homeland

22. SERGEI PROKOFIEV

Ten years after the birth of Béla Bartók, a bright-eyed baby boy was born in Sontsovka, Russia. The Prokofievs named their child Sergei Sergeyevich to distinguish him from his father, Sergei Alexeyevich. They called him Seryozha for short. From the beginning, he heard serious music, his mother being a pianist who specialized in Beethoven and Chopin. She soon granted him the privilege of sitting beside her and playing whatever he liked in the upper two octaves while she practiced her Hanon.

When he was five years old, the boy improvised his first composition. The piece was supposed to be in F major, but it contained no B-flat. This was due, he later explained, not to a love for the Lydian mode but to the fear of playing a black note. He called the piece "The Hindu Gallop," as he had heard his family discussing the famine in India during its composition. He and his mother worked together on the notation. They also played a march he had written for four hands.

After seeing two operas at the Bolshoi Theatre in Moscow, Seryozha wrote a three-act opera with six scenes. He called it "The Giant." Performed first at his home, it was presented the following summer at his uncle's estate. For some time, he and his cousins, with their friends, had been making up plays, raiding the attic for costumes and props. Other activities included playing games, walking on stilts, riding horseback, swimming, playing chess, gardening, reading, and solving problems in mathematics. He delved into carpentry in order to build a doll house.

When he was nearly eleven, Seryozha studied theory in Moscow. That same year, the Prokofievs invited a young conservatory professor to spend the summer with them. With Glière's help, the child wrote several piano pieces he called "ditties" and a symphony. When a former conservatory director examined this opus, he suggested that the harmony might be too ordinary. The comment scored a bull's eye, being directly responsible for some of the unusual harmonies that flowed from Prokofiev's pen.

At the age of thirteen, Sergei Prokofiev passed the entrance exams to the St. Petersburg Conservatory. He submitted a symphony, four operas, two sonatas, and several piano pieces to the examiners, one of whom-- Rimsky-Korsakov--became an instructor of his. Sergei was a rugged individualist, as was Debussy. A kind of running feud existed with some of the teachers.

The most heroic struggle proved to be one waged with Annette Essipov. She had heard Prokofiev perform in a student recital and invited him to join her class. For about two years, pupil and celebrated teacher battled each other. One day, she could stand his careless playing no longer. She issued an ultimatum: "Either you put your hands on the keyboard as I tell you or you leave the class!" Knowing who was right, the pupil gave in and began to work at becoming one of Russia's great pianists.

Prokofiev enjoyed the "Evenings of Contemporary Music" held on Thursdays in a poorly lit piano shop. Here, composers played Bach, their own compositions, and other music not often heard, such as that of Debussy and Ravel. The Russian favorite was Scriabin, and Sergei became an enthusiastic fan of his. He also idolized the music of Sergei Rachmaninoff, who was destined to become one of the world's renowned pianists.

These two musicians met for the first time when Rachmaninoff played at a memorial concert for Scriabin. The older musician heard Prokofiev perform on two occasions, but nearly twenty years went by before Sergei finally saw Rachmaninoff applauding his efforts. This occurred as he took a bow for his ballet *L'Enfant prodigue* in Paris.

At the age of twenty, Prokofiev wrote his first piano concerto. All the critics were not enthusiastic about his performance of it, but the audience liked both the music and the rendition.

The second concerto, written soon after the first, did not meet with the same success. A critic for the St. Petersburg *Gazette* wrote, "He takes his place at the piano and seems to be either dusting the keys or striking high or low notes at random. He has a sharp, dry touch. The public is bewildered. Some indignant murmurs are audible. . . . The hall empties. . . . The young artist concludes his concerto with a relentless discordant combination of brasses. The audience is scandalized. The majority hiss. With a mocking bow, Prokofiev resumes his seat and plays an encore." The concerto later went up in smoke, literally--it was burned by accident and had to be rewritten.

Sergei graduated from the St. Petersburg Conservatory in piano and conducting in 1914. He won the Rubinstein prize, a grand piano, by playing his own First Piano Concerto. On the commencement program, he played this concerto and then reappeared to conduct the orchestra because he'd also won the conducting prize. His proud mother applauded from the front row and rewarded her son with a trip to the country of his choice. He selected England. Here he met the famous impressario of the Russian ballet, Sergei Diaghilev, with whom he later collaborated.

In 1918, Prokofiev set out for the United States. In a trip that he described as "uneventful," he crossed Russia and Siberia. The train, stopped frequently by robbers, eventually met up with an entire Czechoslovak army. The pianist gave concerts in Tokyo and Yokohama and spent some time in Honolulu before arriving at White Island in San Francisco Bay. After being interned for three days, he was permitted to leave for New York.

Prokofiev gave his first concert in Aeolian Hall. Except for a taste of Rachmaninoff and Scriabin, he offered only his own music. The audience, accustomed to the faultless playing of Rachmaninoff, raised their eyebrows at the wrong notes they heard. Their idol sat in *his* seat like a statue, neither smiling nor applauding. Reviewers described Prokofiev's music as "Bolshevism," "an orgy of dissonant sounds," "Russian chaos." One critic gave simple instructions on how to compose such cacophony: "Write anything that comes into your head. . . . Then change all the accidentals, putting flats in place of sharps, and vice versa, and the thing's done." Some decided his mechanical style indicated he must be made of steel. The elevator operator in his hotel read this. One day he gave in to temptation and took hold of the composer's arm, murmuring reverently, "Steel muscles!"

Chicago treated Prokofiev more charitably, and there he received a commission to write an opera. The project ran into numerous obstacles, but Mary Garden finally staged his *Love for Three Oranges*. The "March" from this opera became a popular request from his audiences--somewhat to his ultimate chagrin.

His bout with the combined forces of scarlet fever, diptheria, and a throat ulcer spurred one admirer to action. She sent a bouquet with a note that read, "I thought you were dying, so I sent you these roses."

On his second tour of the United States, Prokofiev included California, where he met a charming young Cuban singer who spoke Russian. Lina became his wife, and they settled in a small town in the Bavarian Alps before moving to Paris.

The musician worked diligently, much to the satisfaction of his mother, who came to live with the couple. Prokofiev preferred composing but gave many concerts all over Europe. For these he had to "cram." Some of the apartment neighbors did not appreciate this and annoyed him by wrapping on the walls. So, he bought lumber and nails and hammered away as though engaged in the legitimate business of building bookshelves. Relief swept over the neighborhood when he returned to practicing the piano.

Serge Koussevitsky, conductor of the Moscow Symphony, performed some of Prokofiev's music. He also published it. Later in Paris, he conducted the exciting Third Piano Concerto with the composer at the piano. After being named conductor of the Boston Symphony, Koussevitsky continued to program Prokofiev and arranged for him to tour with the symphony in the United States. Sergei and Lina gave joint concerts of Russian music for modern-music societies in several cities. Other successful U.S. tours followed.

As time passed, Prokofiev found himself thinking more and more about the land of his birth. In 1933, he decided to return to Russia. He wrote music for the movie "Lieutenant Kije" and continued the concert tours. Finally, he moved his family. Happy to have his two boys with him, he composed *Peter and the Wolf* in one week, orchestrating it in another. Then came *Music for Children*, twelve piano pieces that include "Tag," "Grasshopper's Parade," and "Little Fairy Tale."

By the beginning of World War II, Prokofiev had divorced Lina and married a young language student, Myra Mendelson. She worked with him on the librettos for some of his operas. Because of the war, the two were sent to safety with other artists. Four trainloads of them left Moscow bound for a quiet village in the Caucasus Mountains. They moved several times and eventually arrived at the Ivanovo Rest Home.

Here, Prokofiev found his former conservatory pal, Miaskovsky, and his former tutor, Glière. Shostakovich, Khatchaturian, and Kabalevsky were also in the group. Sergei, always bubbling with energy, decided some of the men were taking the name of the place literally. He stirred up interest in walking and playing tennis or volleyball. Every evening, he called for reports on what had been composed during the day. "Well, boys," he would start out, "and what have you knocked out today?" His accomplishments invariably took first prize. Composed during this summer were his Eighth Piano Sonata, the Fifth Symphony, an orchestration of his ballet *Cinderella*, and numerous smaller works.

Like so many musicians, Prokofiev loved nature. He enjoyed tramping about this huge farm with its fields of rye, its cows, pigs, and eight thousand chickens and ducks. He loved the birds and their songs, the beautiful clouds and the sunsets. At five o'clock each day, he knocked on Kabalevsky's door and they set out on the "large tour around the world," weather permitting.

Along the route, Prokofiev checked several ant hills, admiring the organization and industry of the ants. One day, he found an old shoe which he placed on one of the hills so the ants could make "wonderful rooms." He adopted a small stray dog that vaguely resembled a Pomeranian. Each noon after dinner, he passed a plate for food donations for the dog. He made friends with the children in town by playing games with them and giving them candy. When they saw him, they would cry, "Here comes our uncle," and rush out to meet him.

When Prokofiev conducted his Fifth Symphony in Moscow, it met with instant approval. At the reception afterwards, while standing at the head of the stairs, he had a slight heart attack and fell down the stairs. The resultant concussion hampered the activity of this dynamic, *agitato*-type individual for the next eight years. Frequently, his composing could be limited to an hour, a half hour, or a mere twenty minutes at a time. He strained at the bit constantly, but never lost his inherent optimism--nor did he give in to his severe headaches and attacks of dizziness. He made only one concession, that of moving to the country.

Even here, Sergei Prokofiev could not completely forget his competitive spirit. He named each of his chickens and organized races at feeding time. An older rooster called "Boiler" almost always won. With his usual concern for the underdog, he gave extra bread to the "lady hen" who invariably came in last. At one time, he owned a timid mongrel he referred to as an "Iceland Wolf."

Shortly after his Sixth Symphony received the blessing of the critics, an explosion rocked the composer's peaceful existence. The Central Committee of the Communist Party issued a decree on music. Prokofiev was accused of writing music that showed the corrupt influence of the West. Like a cat surprised from an unexpected source, he arched his back and prepared to fight. After considering the power of the enemy and the fact that he had a wife, he finally apologized and walked away. But he went on writing as he always had.

A stroke sent Prokofiev back to the hospital, helpless and unable to speak. Almost by sheer willpower, he managed to regain his speech. At home once more, he wrote *Winter Bonfire*, a suite for boys' choir and orchestra. Soon, he returned to the hospital and then entered a sanatorium. At long last, permitted to work for twenty minutes, he felt "like a human being again."

Prokofiev now began an oratorio titled *Stand Up for Peace*. Of the composition, he wrote: "it was born from life, from its boiling state . . . from everything that disturbs me as well as everybody else." And he added: "In this oratorio I have tried to express my feelings about peace and war, my conviction that there will be no war, that the people all over the world will stand up for peace, will save our civilization, our children and our future." For this composition, Prokofiev received the 1951 Stalin Prize.

On his sixtieth birthday, the composer was honored with concerts throughout Russia. He attempted to attend the Moscow celebration but was just not up to it. Somehow, he got to the première of his Seventh Symphony. The audience cheered for him much as Brahms' admirers had applauded *his* farewell appearance.

On the day that Stalin died, March 5, 1953, Prokofiev had been revising his ballet, *The Stone Flower*. He suffered a cerebral hemorrhage and died a few hours later, leaving a rich legacy of original, vital music. Included are seven ballets; eight operas; seven symphonies; five piano concertos (including one for the left hand alone); two violin concertos; nine piano sonatas; and other piano, choral and chamber works.

Prokofiev's music is full of delightful surprises. A pioneer who liked to shock his listeners, he often followed simple chords with dissonances, or harmonized a simple tune in an unusual manner. He used diatonic scales primarily but added chromaticism, also. He took a special fancy to the interval of the augmented fourth.

Prokofiev's piano playing reflected his remarkable vitality--his extraordinary drive. He treated the piano as a percussion instrument, using minimal pedal and steel-like tone.

Sergei Prokofiev dressed conservatively and neatly, was methodical, efficient, and always on time. He faced frequent rebuff from teachers, performers, critics, the public, and his country. Finally, his own constitution failed him. Yet he never failed to accentuate the positive. He seemed to regard adversity as a challenge that constantly tilted him to the UP side of life's seesaw.

Sergei Prokofiev at age 10 (copy of "The Giant" on piano).

At an early age, the child received a green notebook from his mother, who advised him to write everything down. Prokofiev kept many journals, as did Clara Schumann. The above illustration is from his autobiography, *Prokofiev By Prokofiev*, Copyright 1979 by Doubleday & Company, Inc.

23.   GERSHWIN and COPLAND

George Gershwin's world revolved around the city of New York. It turned from the sidewalks of the Lower East Side to Broadway and, finally, to Carnegie Hall.

Parents of both Gershwin and Copland had emigrated to this country from Russia and had settled in Brooklyn. But six weeks after George's birth in 1898, the Gershwins moved to Manhattan. This was the first of numerous moves about the city. After both parents involved themselves in business ventures, George roamed the city streets in his free time. He was tough, usually winning fights, and he became "the roller skating champion of Seventh Street."

At the age of six, he would stand outside a penny arcade on 125th Street, barefoot and in overalls. Years later, he still remembered being captivated by Rubinstein's "Melody in F," but he had decided that music was for girls. He found his first girlfriend at the age of nine; she played the piano and sang.

George was ten when he happened to hear a student at his school playing the violin. Impressed, he spent the entire afternoon in a downpour, trying to find the talented violinist who later became famous. They became close friends with music as a common interest, although Max Rosen refused George's offer to serve as his accompanist. He thought George was not equipped for a career in music.

Gershwin was twelve when an upright piano was hoisted through the living room window so that his brother Ira could take lessons. George rushed to the piano and, to everyone's surprise, played a popular piece he had learned at a neighbor's house. Ira soon gave up the lessons, being more interested in words than in notes. Later he wrote many of the lyrics for George's songs.

When George found a teacher who recognized his ability, he learned the standard repertoire, including music of Chopin, Liszt, and Debussy. He attended concerts, wrote and edited a magazine, and took private lessons in theory and harmony.

George Gershwin left high school at the age of fifteen to work as a "piano pounder" for a sheet-music publisher. He demonstrated popular songs for prospective customers. Playing pieces over and over led to experimentation with harmonies and improvisation of his own accompaniments. He also cut a few piano rolls for player pianos, and some of these rolls included his own music.

Five years after leaving school, George wrote the music for his first Broadway show. Al Jolson recorded his song "Swanee," and George Gershwin's flight to stardom took off toward the sky.

Gershwin wrote countless musicals. Some were striking successes, and some were failures. He filled numerous "Tune Books" with song ideas for both popular and serious music. On January 27, 1923, he started work on his *Rhapsody in Blue*, which was to be played in New York's Aeolian Hall on February 12 with Paul Whiteman's band. The composer lacked the time to write out all the solo piano parts, so he improvised some of them, as Mozart had done with some of his own works. The audience applauded wildly; critics were less enthusiastic, although they mentioned his melodic gift, ingenious rhythms, and creativity. His piano technique impressed everyone.

Walter Damrosch, the noted conductor, attended the concert and immediately asked the New York Symphony Society to commission a piano concerto. MacDowell and Gottschalk had both knocked at the door to Symphony Hall with their inclusion of American music, but George Gershwin swung it open. The country's best-known magazine for piano teachers, *The Etude*, that same year published an issue that dealt with what they called "the jazz problem." To the staff's consternation, a survey revealed that many prominent musicians welcomed the invasion. Sixty-five years later, in 1989, Meet the Composer, Inc. announced a $250,000 grant (from the Rockefeller Foundation and AT&T) to commission jazz compositions in all disciplines.

Gershwin signed the contract for his piano concerto in April, with the first performance scheduled for December. He hunted up some books on musical form and orchestration. Then he left for London, where he was involved with a musical and a concert. He jotted down ideas in his Tune Book as they occurred to him. After his return to New York by way of Paris, he wrote the concerto in three months and orchestrated it in another month. Audiences loved it, but critics were, as usual, divided. He played his concerto in Washington, Philadelphia, and Baltimore, as well as in New York.

That same year, Gershwin worked on preludes for the piano, finally publishing three of them. These employ American dance rhythms, such as the tango and the Charleston, much as Chopin's music often made reference to the Polish dances. Later in London, George recorded his preludes for the Columbia Gramophone Company.

In the spring of 1928, Gershwin went to Paris, making his fifth and final crossing of the Atlantic. He met many famous composers there, asking three of them for composition lessons. Ravel, Stravinsky, and Nadia Boulanger all turned him down, apparently afraid of interfering with his natural ability. In Paris, as at home, he performed his music at parties, sometimes playing until dawn. When Prokofiev heard Gershwin at one of these gatherings, he predicted a great future for the composer, providing he could forget money-making and parties.

George attended many concerts in Paris. One of them at the *Theatre National de l'Opéra* included Copland's *Cortége Macabre* followed by Gershwin's *Concerto en fa*. The composer worked on *An American in Paris*, finding several Paris taxi-horns to use in the tone poem. He also purchased an eight-volume collection of Debussy's works for piano. On December 13, 1928, Walter Damrosch conducted the Philharmonic-Symphony Society of New York in Carnegie Hall. The program included *An American in Paris*.

The following summer, Gershwin conducted his music at New York's Lewisohn Stadium. Enthusiastic about this newest accomplishment, he would often conduct opening-night performances of his musicals.

Gershwin continued to compose, to perform, and to study. He took up painting and acquired an extensive collection of art. He delved into literature and became interested in science. In 1934, he had his own radio show called "Music by Gershwin." He thoroughly researched everything. When he started working on the folk opera *Porgy and Bess,* he spent nearly six weeks at Folly Beach outside Charleston, South Carolina. He attended church services and prayer meetings, listening to spirituals. Even here, he entertained, sometimes playing for the blacks when they were supposed to be singing for him. George always sat down at the piano when he was asked to play.

George Gershwin's career ended in Hollywood where he wrote music for motion pictures. Still hoping to return to his beloved New York City, he died of a brain tumor at the age of thirty-eight.

Porgy and Bess proved itself to be Gershwin's crowning achievement. A noted authority on Arican-American music called the composer the Abraham Lincoln of Negro music. Moses Smith, the renowned critic of Boston's *Evening Transcript*, admitted that George Gershwin must be considered a "serious" composer.

*   *   *

Aaron Copland described the Brooklyn street on which he lived for twenty years, as "drab." He added that it was not the kind of street from which you would expect a musician to emerge. Born in 1900, Aaron was thirteen years old when he came up with the idea of studying music seriously. He'd had a few lessons on the piano from his sister Laurine, and an older brother played the violin. Selections from ragtime pieces and operas were sometimes played at home, but his parents were not musical. His father owned a department store in Brooklyn, New York. Neither parent was enthusiastic over the idea of spending more money for music lessons. They felt they had already wasted enough on the four older children. But they finally gave in.

Aaron made his own arrangements for piano lessons with a local teacher. During high school years, he borrowed four-hand music from the library and played it with a friend. He also loved reading, Walt Whitman being a favorite author. His sisters taught him to dance, and a maid predicted that "Mr. Aaron" would one day be "swingin' in circles." He heard Percy Grainger play the Grieg Piano Concerto and was impressed.

At the age of seventeen, after three years of lessons, Aaron played Paderewski's *Polonaise in B* in a recital at Wanamaker auditorium in Manhattan. On the way to the stage, he was startled when his teacher "boxed his ears" and told him not to be nervous. This, he later learned, was to give him something to think about so that he wouldn't be nervous.

At about this time, Aaron began to study harmony. Like so many budding composers, he soon discovered he would rather write music *his* way than follow the rules. Opus 1, *The Cat and the Mouse*, proved too modern for his harmony teacher. From then on, the student wrote two kinds of music: the type written to please the instructor, and the kind that came from his heart.

After playing the piano for two summers in the Catskill Mountains, Copland learned of a music school abroad for Americans. It would open the following summer, in 1921, in the Palace of Fontainbleau near Paris. He enrolled immediately--his name was first on the list. Unfortunately, his composition teacher there bore a close resemblance to his former harmony teacher. When a friend recommended studying with a Mademoiselle Boulanger, Copland showed no interest After all, who had ever heard of a famous female composer? But he visited her class, changed his mind, and became, apparently, her "first full-fledged American composition student." Through her, he met Koussevitsky. Later, this charming, talented teacher would lure young composers from all over the world.

In France, Copland heard music from everywhere. He sat high in the balcony of the Paris Opéra for the *Concerts Koussevitsky*. These presented many new works by contemporaries such as Prokofiev, Falla, and Bartók. Copland himself wrote several motets, a passacaglia for piano, a rondino for string quartet, and a ballet titled *Grohg*. When he played *The Cat and the Mouse* at Fontainebleau, Durand heard it. During the intermission, he offered forty dollars for the right to publish it.

Returning to America in June of 1924, Copland worked on an organ concerto. Nadia Boulanger had asked him to write one for her upcoming American tour. At the same time, he played piano in a Milford, Pennsylvania, hotel. That fall, he performed *The Cat and the Mouse* and his *Passacaglia* in the League of Composers November concert. And Walter Damrosch conducted Copland's *Symphony for Organ and Orchestra* with Mademoiselle Boulanger at the organ. Soon afterwards, the Boston Symphony presented the *Organ Symphony* under its new conductor, Serge Koussevitsky.

This friend of contemporary composers now suggested that the League of Composers commission a work by Copland. Aaron had tried to set up a studio in Manhattan. But despite having sent out announcements, he heard no knocking at the door. After receiving the first Guggenheim fellowship given to a composer, he went to work composing the commissioned *Music for the Theatre* at the MacDowell Colony. In an attempt to write "American" music, he used jazz in this work and also in the *Concerto for Piano* that followed.

It was also Koussevitsky who suggested that Copland write a piano concerto, since he could then play it himself. The Boston Symphony introduced it in Boston and New York City. A Boston critic wrote: "With no effort at all the listener visualizes a jazz dance hall next door to a poultry yard." At the rehearsal for a Hollywood Bowl performance, some of the musicians hissed.

Copland never seemed to take criticism personally but worked at educating audiences and young people. He gave lectures and wrote books aimed toward a better understanding of "modern music." His *What to Listen for in Music* offers a painless dose of music appreciation for all ages. Written in an informal style, it is a publication guaranteed to increase the joy of playing and listening to music. Other books include *Our New Music*, *Copland on Music*, *Music and Imaginations*, and *Copland 1900 through 1942* (written with Vivian Perlis).

Copland taught for twenty-five years at Tanglewood's Berkshire Center in Massachusetts, showing interest and concern for his students. He helped to organize Cos Cob Press, which published contemporary music and paid composers 50-percent, instead of 10-percent, royalties.

Aaron Copland did much to introduce American music to European audiences. When he played his concerts in Frankfurt in 1927, the musicians gathered around the piano to learn how to play the jazz rhythms. He spent several months in Mexico and in South America, where he was sent by the State Department on a good-will tour.

The second visit to Mexico gave Copland an opportunity to "practice" his conducting, thus initiating another career. Later, he conducted orchestras in Rome, London, Paris, Munich, Trieste, and Zurich before finally taking up the baton in the United States. At the Ravinia Festival, he conducted the Chicago Symphony in an open-air concert. He was invited to return there many times. (On one stormy evening, the heavens responded to his down beat with a fortissimo clap of thunder. This broke up audience and musicians alike, forcing a new beginning.) The maestro conducted over one hundred symphony orchestras.

Copland's life was a full one. He was a pianist, composer, conductor, teacher, lecturer, and author. He did not, however, live on Easy Street all his life. In September of 1938, his checkbook showed a balance of $6.93. He was nearly forty years old before royalties from *Billy the Kid* convinced his mother that the piano lessons had been worthwhile.

Copland's work includes an opera for high school students, *The Second Hurricane*. His *Outdoor Overture* is included in the Music Educators National Conference contest repertoire for orchestras. He wrote pieces for children in the contemporary idiom: *Sunday Afternoon Music* and *The Young Pioneers*. Ballets *Rodeo, Billy the Kid,* and *Appalachian Spring* depict the American scene, as do some of his other well-known works. He wrote scores for eight films, spending some time in Hollywood and winning an Academy Award for "The Heiress."

Copland found time to write music wherever he happened to be. He completed his Piano Sonata in Santiago de Chile. Part of his Clarinet Concerto for Benny Goodman he composed in Rio de Janeiro. He worked on his Third Symphony in Mexico, finishing it later in a converted barn near Tanglewood. He spent fourteen summers in this barn, and it was here that he delved into the twelve-tone technique found in the Piano Quartet of 1950. He continued to utilize this compositional approach in his *Piano Fantasy* and the *Connotations for Orchestra*.

Aaron Copland won many awards and received many honors. There were many November concerts, celebrations, and cakes following his fiftieth birthday. On this birthday, at a dinner party at the home of Claire Reis, director of the League of Composers, the honored guest asked how to cut a birthday cake. Celebrations of his 85th birthday included an all-Copland program by the New York Philharmonic on public television.

Perhaps what Aaron Copland treasured most was the affection in which he was held by so many, young and old. Vincent Persichetti once said, "I would like Aaron Copland very much even if he were not a composer."

Aaron Copland died on December 2, 1990, not quite three weeks after his ninetieth birthday.

Emma Lou Diemer (b. 1927)

24. HOVHANESS, DELLO JOIO, PERSICHETTI, and DIEMER

Alan Hovhaness was born in 1911 in the Boston suburb of Somerville, Massachusetts. His father, who taught chemistry, was Armenian and his mother Scottish. At the age of four, Alan composed a short piece for organ that he notated on an eleven-line staff. His mother refused to play it on their small harmonium. The child then gave up music until he was seven; but he kept hearing it in his head, and he improvised before he had formal lessons.

After moving to nearby Arlington, Alan took piano lessons from a teacher who encouraged his composing. By the time he reached thirteen, he had written two operas as well as many shorter pieces.

Hovhaness spent a year and a half at Tufts College before enrolling at the New England Conservatory of Music. Here he studied counterpoint and composition with Frederick Converse. Hovhaness "appreciated Converse very much as a teacher, composer and a wonderful person," as had many other NEC students.

In 1933, a Hovhaness symphony won the Samuel Endicott prize for composition. (This symphony was later destroyed along with hundreds of other early compositions.) *Exile*, a symphony written in 1936, became Symphony No.1. In manuscript form, it may have saved its composer from jail: Hovhaness was in Manchester, New Hampshire, on holiday with a friend, the late Roy Stoughton, another composer interested in Oriental music. The two were fascinated by Manchester's electric street cars with their stained glass windows. They spent a lot of time on them. While riding in the mill district, they were arrested. The police suspected them of being labor agitators. At the police station, they appropriated Alan's large music case only to discover several music scores, including that of the *"Exile Symphony."* The embarrassed police promptly released the two musicians. The symphony was first played in England by the British Broadcasting Company. Its conductor, Leslie Heward, called the composer a genius and predicted a great future for him.

From 1940 to 1947, Hovhaness served as organist at an Armenian church in Watertown, Mass. He taught privately and accompanied. The Armenian church music, with its modes and individual melodies, influenced his compositions. He wrote *Twelve Armenian Folk Songs* for piano and *Armenian Rhapsodies* for strings.

After attending a performance by dancers and musicians from India, Hovhaness began a study of Eastern religions and philosophies. The Eastern influence soon appeared in his music. His *Lousadzak* (Coming of Light), a concerto for piano and orchestra, presents the sounds of Eastern instruments as played by instruments of the West. In 1945, he presented this music as part of an all-Hovhaness program in New York City. A few years later, after three years on the Boston Conservatory faculty, he moved to Manhattan.

In the 1950s, Hovhaness's Symphony No. 2, *The Mysterious Mountain*, was premiered by the Houston Symphony under Leopold Stokowski. Hugh Ross conducted his *Easter Cantata* and *Magnificat* at Tanglewood. "These," the composer writes, "were happy occasions." (The summer spent as a student at Tanglewood in 1942 had been marred by a disagreement with Copland and Bernstein.)

In 1959, Alan Hovhaness began a world tour that included India and Japan. At the Tokyo airport, he received a hero's welcome. He appeared on local television stations and conducted the Tokyo Symphony in a performance of his music. He played the piano in Tokyo and other Japanese cities, in Madras, India, and Honolulu. Later, he performed in France and Germany and served as composer-in-residence at the University of Hawaii.

After receiving a Rockefeller grant for music research, Hovhaness traveled to Korea and again to Japan. His Symphony No.16, inspired by paintings of rivers and mountains in the National Museum of Korea, had its first performance in Seoul, Korea. It is written for Korean instruments and strings. In Tokyo, he wrote the libretto and music for a one-act opera he titled *Spirit of the Avalanche.*

Alan Hovhaness, one of America's most prolific composers, has written music for almost every instrument and medium. His *Fantasy of Japanese Woodprints* is for xylophone and orchestra. There are concertos for numerous instruments. He uses unusual combinations of elements, counterpoint, complex rhythms and special effects such as bells and timpani and marimba sticks inside the piano. An excellent pianist himself, he strives to make his music playable. He has written for film documentaries and ballets. Some of his music reveals an interest in the Baroque. There's a sextet for alto recorder, string quartet, and harpsichord; a duet for violin and harpsichord; modal fugues and canons. For his daughter, harpsichordist Jean Nandi, he has written several harpsichord sonatas.

Hovhaness, married to the Japanese soprano, Hinako Fugihara, now lives in Seattle, Washington. Still responsive to mountains as symbols of man's attempt to reach God, his Symphony No. 67 (1991) is inspired by the Cascade Mountains and Glacier Peak.

Deep religious mysticism pervades much of this composer's music. His fondness for Oriental music stems in part from the fact that it has a tonal center. The essence of beauty, he feels, is simplicity. This establishes a difficult goal for the artist--but one in which composer Alan Hovhaness firmly believes.

*   *   *

Many musicians gravitate to New York City; not many are born there. One exception is Edward MacDowell, and another is Norman Dello Joio, born in 1913. Descended from a long line of Italian church musicians, his father came to the United States early in the twentieth century. He brought with him a love for Italian opera, and his son heard it played and sung at home in the evenings. Soon he was able to pick out arias on the piano. His father gave him lessons in piano, organ, and theory, and they played duet arrangements of classical music. Later, Norman studied organ with his godfather, Pietro Yon, organist of St. Patrick's Cathedral. Playing the piano came easily for the boy--he sightread well--and he enjoyed writing music. He also had time for his favorite sport--baseball.

At the age of twelve, Norman Dello Joio assisted his father at the church organ. Two years later, he had his own church position and was soon playing in jazz bands. At the age of twenty, he directed his own band. And he entered the Institute of Musical Art where he studied harmony, music theory, piano, and organ. He won the Elizabeth Sprague Coolidge one-thousand-dollar award for his piano trio.

When he was twenty-four years old, Dello Joio began to take composing seriously. In 1939, he entered the Juilliard graduate school, where he studied composition with Bernard Wagenaar. The following year, when the Berkshire Music Center opened at Tanglewood, Norman was among those present. Classes met in an old boathouse, and students included Leonard Bernstein and Lucas Foss. At eleven o'clock each morning, a bell rang and the class took time to cool off with a swim in the lake. But they also took their lessons seriously. Impressed by the teaching of Paul Hindemith, Dello Joio studied with him at Yale University during the winters. As a result, he withdrew some of his earlier compositions, including the one-thousand-dollar trio.

In December of 1946, the composer played *Ricercari for Piano and Orchestra* with the New York Philharmonic under George Szell. The concert took place in Carnegie Hall. Critics praised both composition and performer. His *Variations*, *Chaconne*, and *Finale* won the Music Critics Circle award for the 1948 season's best symphonic work. He has won many other awards, including a Pulitzer Prize for *Meditations on Ecclesiastes* for strings. His score for *Scenes from the Louvre* won an Emmy from the National Academy of Arts and Sciences.

In 1958, Dello Joio became professor of composition at the Mannes College of Music in New York City. A few years later, he was sent by the U.S. State Department to Romania, Bulgaria, and the Soviet Union as cultural representative. In Hawaii, he served as U.S. representative to the Festival of the Arts. In 1972, he assumed the position of acting dean of fine and applied arts at Boston University.

For several years, Dello Joio served as chairman of the Policy committee of the Contemporary Music Project for Creativity in Music Education. He himself had conceived the idea of sponsoring young composers to write new music for high school ensembles. The Ford Foundation supported this project.

Dello Joio has written operas; ballets; chamber and orchestral music; band, organ, and piano music; songs and masses. He uses modern harmonies and rhythms often in Baroque form. Much of his music is religious, using Gregorian chant. It also reveals a flair for the dramatic. *New York Profiles* is a suite of pieces that musically describe seven New York City places of interest. The "Cloisters" employs Gregorian chant, and "Grant's Tomb" quotes from the "Battle Hymn of the Republic." For jazz artist Artie Shaw, Dello Joio wrote a *Concertante for Clarinet and Orchestra.*

Piano music includes preludes, nocturnes, three piano sonatas, *Fantasy and Variations for the Piano and Orchestra*, the *Ricercari,* and *Concerto for 2 Pianos and Orchestra.* His *Suite for the Young* and *Lyric Pieces for the Young* are favorites with piano students and their teachers. For two pianists who like to make music together, he has written *Family Album* and *Christmas Music.*

National Public Radio celebrated the eightieth birthday of Norman Dello Joio on *Performance Today* with an interview of the composer and recordings of some of his music.

*   *   *

Vincent Persichetti spent his entire life in the Philadelphia area, but his music premiered all over the United States and in Japan, Turkey, France, and Poland. His Italian father and German mother came to this country as children. Neither parent was musical, but they supported their son in his talent and love for music. Vincent began to study piano in 1920 at the age of five. Soon he added theory, composition, organ, double bass, and tuba to his studies.

When he was eleven years old, he served as church organist, staff pianist at a radio station, accompanist, and double bass player in orchestras. He also delved into composing, his earliest published works being written at the age of fourteen. At sixteen, he became organist--and later choir director--at the Arch Street Presbyterian Church in Philadelphia. He held this position for eighteen years.

Persichetti received his Bachelor of Music degree from Combs Conservatory, where he was made head of the theory and composition departments. He studied conducting at Curtis Institute with Fritz Reiner and piano with Olga Samaroff at the Philadelphia Conservatory.

One day when he arrived unprepared for his piano lesson, he decided to play, on the piano, a Brahms organ prelude and fugue while reading from the organ score. Impressed, Samaroff suggested he write out what he had played. Concert pianist Eugene List happened on to it and played it in public. A critic liked it, and it was accepted by a publisher.

Persichetti received his master's degree and doctorate from the Philadelphia Conservatory. He also studied composition briefly with a pupil of Nadia Boulanger, Roy Harris. Persichetti had second thoughts about some of his earlier music, just as Hovhaness and Dello Joio had about some of their early works. Persichetti destroyed the pieces he no longer liked.

At the age of twenty-six, Persichetti became head of Philadelphia Conservatory's theory and composition departments. He married a pianist, Dorothea Flanagan. She played his music in public, and they played four-hand and two-piano music together.

Six years later, Persichetti was appointed to the Juilliard faculty. He eventually became head of the composition department of this famous music school. In 1952, he was named director of the music publishing company Elkan-Vogel, Inc.

Vincent Persichetti won many prestigious awards. These were not always for music. At the age of nine, he won the Drexel Mathematical Award. Years later, he won trophies for sailing. An artist and sculptor, he also received numerous fellowships and commissions. As composer, lecturer, and guest conductor he visited more than two hundred universities. He wrote a treatise titled *Twentieth Century Harmony: Creative Aspects and Practice*, and coauthored a biography of William Schuman. In 1978, he served as the U.S. representative for ASCAP at an International Composers meeting in Armenia and the Soviet Union.

Persichetti's published works number over 150. Two premières took place in Philadelphia on the same day. On April 20, 1945, Eugene Ormandy conducted the Philadelphia Orchestra in *Fables for Narrator and Orchestra*; and the Curtis Quintet performed his *Pastoral for Woodwind Quintet*. Persichetti wrote a variety of chamber works, band, vocal, and choral works. His music for orchestra includes nine symphonies. The popular Symphony No. 6 is written for band. The seventh symphony, *Liturgic*, is religious in character, using material from his *Hymns and Responses for the Church Year*. The ninth symphony, commissioned by the Philadelphia Orchestra, was

Orchestra, was written in Rome, Italy. His one-act opera, for which he wrote the libretto, is called *The Sibyl* (a parable of Chicken Little).

Self-portrait by Vincent Persichetti
Courtesy of Theodore Presser Company

Persichetti wrote for various solo instruments, including organ, harpsichord, and piano: sonatas, serenades, a piano concerto and a concertino for piano and orchestra, a four-hand concerto, and three volumes of *Poems*. He published *A Little Poem Book*, *A Little Recorder Book*, and *A Little Harpsichord Book*. Having written nine harpsichord sonatas, Vincent Persichetti contributed more than any other composer to the twentieth-century revival of the harpsichord

In honor of Persichetti's seventieth birthday, Boston-area schools, including Harvard and Radcliffe, offered a week-long celebration. There were lectures/demonstrations, concerts, and discussions. At one of the concerts, two pianists played *The Appalachian Christmas Carols*. The composer conducted some of his own music and was given, as he reported, "a birthday cake with lit candles."

Vincent Persichetti died of lung cancer on August 14, 1987.

*   *   *

Emma Lou Diemer, born in 1927 in Kansas City, Missouri, composed her first pieces for piano at the age of six. She wrote imagery-filled music such as "Church Bells" and, in the key of A minor, "Santa Lost His Toy Bag." At the age of ten, she finally learned to read music in order to accompany her sister and twin brothers, all of whom played different instruments. By the time she reached thirteen, she was writing piano concertos and playing the organ in church.

On Sunday afternoons, Emma Lou listened to the New York Philharmonic broadcasts on radio. She particularly enjoyed the music of Chopin, Debussy, and Gershwin, although she wrote, "I have always loved the music of many classical and popular composers, but prefer to write my own music, to 'do it my way' as the song goes. In high school I composed at the piano before going to classes in the morning, enjoying the privacy of the quiet house and concentrated time to work out musical ideas."

Even before becoming familiar with the twelve-tone technique, the young composer had decided her music did not have to be tonal. She admits enjoying early-music concerts, but she really prefers contemporary music.

Diemer earned her bachelor's and master's degrees at Yale University, where she studied with Paul Hindemith. On a Fulbright scholarship, she studied composition and piano at the Royal Conservatory in Brussels. There, she performed frequently at the American Embassy as pianist/composer and accompanist, making trips to other European cities for concerts. She spent the summers of 1954 and 1955 at Tanglewood.

In 1960, Diemer received the Doctor of Philosophy degree in composition from the Eastman School of Music, where she studied with Hanson, Rogers, Sessions, and Toch.

As composer-in-residence for the Arlington, Virginia, secondary schools--she was the first woman to receive one of these Ford Foundation grants--Diemer published twenty-two compositions. They include *Youth Overture*, *Symphonie Antique*, and *Brass Menagerie Suite for Band*, as well as choral music. Later she served as composition consultant for a Contemporary Music project of the Music Educators National Conference in the public schools of Baltimore, Maryland. For five years, she taught theory and composition at the University of Maryland. When she played her *Fantasie* for the Washington Chapter of the American Guild of Organists, she received high praise for both composition and performance.

In 1971, Emma Lou Diemer was appointed professor of theory and composition at the University of California, Santa Barbara, where she served for twenty years before becoming Professor Emeritus. Organist at the First Presbyterian Church in Santa Barbara, she gives regular concerts, piano programs, and workshops. In 1976, in a concert of keyboard compositions by women composers, she presented her *PIANOHARPSICHORDORGAN*. For this, she prerecorded on each instrument and combined their sounds on tape. She strummed the piano strings with tympani sticks and her fingers; massive harpsichord sounds were produced by striking the keyboard with the entire arm.

As composer-in-residence with the Santa Barbara Symphony, Diemer wrote *Concerto in One Movement for Piano*, which won a

Kennedy Center Friedheim Award and a performance by the National Symphony in 1992.

Diemer's compositions number in the hundreds. She has written for orchestra, band, organ, piano, chorus, solo voice, and chamber ensembles. There are symphonies; concertos for flute, piano, marimba, and harpsichord; overtures; and pieces for carillon. An adventurer, she has experimented with electronic and computer music. Her *Sound Pictures* is a collection of ten pieces that demonstrate contemporary-music techniques for early-intermediate-level piano students. *Space Suite*, commissioned by *Clavier* magazine and published in 1989, presents twelve short, programmatic pieces that move from the simple beauty of "Billions of Stars" to the complexity of "Toward Mars." They display the piano's infinite sound possibilities, offering exciting material for "outer space" recitals.

Diemer composes primarily on commission, although she has written numerous piano pieces that have found their way into various publications: *Monkey Dance* and *Contemplation*, for example. Her *Toccata for Piano* was written for a student's senior recital. She composed *Homage to Cowell, Cage, Crumb, and Czerny* for her piano-department chairman and his wife.

Emma Lou Diemer's music is heard throughout the country. She is featured frequently as composer or performer. Her music has been the subject of five doctoral dissertations and is available in numerous recordings. Since 1962, she has received annual ASCAP Standing Awards.

Concerning her method of composing, Diemer wrote, "I almost always compose at the piano (or lately sometimes at the synthesizer), improvise until I find a usable idea, and depend very much on the process of improvisation for the impetus and development of work." Although she has occasionally written away from the piano, she finds it "more pleasurable to hear the sound of the instrument." She strives for "accessible music that is also well-crafted." And, she finds simplicity both desirable and difficult, as does Hovhaness and many other mature composers.

Emma Lou Diemer is a "doer," a dedicated pioneer in many areas not previously frequented by women. She is still "doing it my way," diligently composing, performing, and recording. Her prescription offered to young people is one that she herself has obviously followed. She wrote, "Young people need to find something at which they can excel, something that will become almost an obsession with them, but it must be a useful and constructive addition to the world around them. Talent and hard work are all that are necessary."

CODA

"Talent and hard work" have supplied the magic lamp and ring for most of these pianists/composers. Although weighed down by many problems-- poor health, poverty, deafness, loneliness--they managed to rise above these difficulties. They believed in themselves and persevered. Not all are remembered for their playing. Some used this talent as a springboard from which to dive into the sea of composing or teaching. None was content to float. Each made waves that still crest around the world.

In the beginning--they all sat down at the piano.